Spiritual Technologies

A USER'S MANUAL

by Edward Stevens

Paulist Press
New York and New Jersey

D1509658

Book design by Nighthawk Design.

Library of Congress Cataloging-in-Publication Data

Stevens, Edward, 1928–
    Spiritual technologies: a user's manual/by Edward Stevens.
      p. cm.
    Includes bibliographical references.
    ISBN 0-8091-3140-4
    1. Spiritual life—Catholic authors—Handbooks, manuals, etc.
  I. Title.
BX2350.2.S7428   1990
248—dc20   89-78449
                                              CIP

Published by Paulist Press
997 Macarthur Boulevard
Mahwah, NJ 07430

Printed and bound in the
United States of America

Contents

I. Introduction

Introduction

My dear brothers and sisters, we are already one. But we imagine that we are not. What we have to recover is our original unity. What we have to be is what we are.

THOMAS MERTON[1]

There are many valid descriptions of the meditative process, and there are many valid techniques for coming to realization. Further, there are many valid descriptions of what realization is. Nowadays, even Buddhist teachers sometimes speak of realizing God! I just happened to use that word God here, but we could just as well use words like "the ground of being" or the "natural state."

SHINZEN[2]

A. Alternative Paths

Yoga means a pathway to becoming what you are meant to be. Different people follow different paths. Some people find their life's quest for fulfillment in devotion to a group and a cause; this is *bhakti yoga,* the path of the devotee. Others pride themselves on being practical and down-to-earth; it is in work and in action that they find their identity and fulfillment; this is *karma yoga,* the path of action. Others still are contemplatives at heart. They seek wisdom and personal fulfillment in the cultivation of their mind, their spirit, and their sensibilities; such is *jnana yoga,* the path of wisdom.

What if you are up to your neck in the world of action, and would like to pay more attention to the spiritual side of things, but don't have the time or the energy? This is a book to help incorporate the life of the spirit into the world of action, to bring wisdom into your *karma*. It is not a book of devotion, *bhakti yoga*. It is *jnana yoga* for people of action.

When people sense, justifiably or not, that they are thrown on their own religious resources, there's not much in the culture to guide them. Religious institutions are out there for anyone to avail themselves of. Objective institutional religion is exoteric, ecumenical, open to all. But the subjective pole of religious experience in American culture remains esoteric, the province of the privileged few, or in the eyes of many, the deluded few. It is even unconstitutional for a group of children to maintain a moment of silence in a public school.

B. Purpose and Point of View of Spiritual Technologies

One purpose of this book is to demystify mysticism. The mystical dimension of religion is not the special province of desert monks, cloistered nuns, or oriental meditation halls. Just as it is human to seek objective salvation or enlightenment in a community, so it is also human to pursue a unique and personal path toward spiritual transformation and enlightenment. They complement each other. Your spiritual faculties are just as much a part of your human makeup as your eyes, your sex, or your ability to do arithmetic. Techniques are available to develop your spiritual powers. No need to go through life as a spiritual basket case. The techniques for cultivating spiritual wisdom and self-transformation are quite straightforward, simple, and available to all.

Mysticism, too, has its pitfalls and excesses as has been pointed out. Also there is an army of would-be gurus and hucksters, along with authentic guides who are responding to the personal religious hunger, often unfulfilled by traditional forms of worship. A second purpose of this book is to offer some suggestions and guidelines for avoiding the pitfalls of spiritual contemplation and for resisting the blandishments of false guides. You the practitioner must be the final arbiter of your own authentic path.

The core of the book is a set of practical techniques for spiritual growth. I have tested them over the past ten years with hundreds of people and modified them in response to feedback about what worked best and what didn't work. I owe a special debt to Anthony de Mello, recently deceased, for his felicitous use of eastern techniques to develop the Ignatian *Spiritual Exercises.* While he is more inclined to speak in Hindu accents with panentheistic assumptions, I have found the naturalistic and apophatic metaphysics of Buddhism more satisfactory for this enterprise, for reasons to be noted later on.[3]

But this is a book about practice rather than theory. You are encouraged to engage in the techniques in an experimental way, to accept them as working hypotheses, to check them against your own experience. Travel lightly. This need not be the conscious "practice of religion," or even of "prayer." Put aside the baggage of religious dogma for a moment. Play with the techniques. Be critical of them even as you enjoy them. The spiritual part of humanity is a natural function to be lived and enjoyed like your other natural functions. To be sure, the spiritual task of self-transformation is not a trivial matter. But this importance need not degenerate into self-importance, or into morbid "seriosity." As for theory, the final section of the book contains short notes on metaphysics for the philosophically inclined.

The first set of techniques are "Awareness" exercises—awareness in the Buddhist sense of *vipassana* meditation techniques. These are aimed at spiritual growth and transformation. They are not merely for relaxation or therapy, though they could have these results too. The second set of techniques are fantasy-based or "Imagination" exercises. One group of these has a genuinely spiritual and transformative purpose. The other group is psychologically rather than spiritually oriented—techniques for making decisions and carrying them out effectively. These latter are included for two reasons. First, effective decision-making, though it is primarily a psychological skill, is a necessary presupposition for spiritual growth. Second, spiritual growth is often confused with psychological growth; viewing spiritual and psychological techniques side by side will help you distinguish between these two areas.

View these techniques as a kind of spiritual tool kit. Experiment with them. Latch on to those that work best for you. By way of introduction, start with the first technique, "Getting Started." After that, try them in any order. Each technique is self-contained. Since they don't logically build on what went before, there is a little bit of repetition. But I try to keep it to a minimum. You are the expert on what you need. And above all, you are the expert on what is working best for you.

While the book focuses on practice more than theory, each technique includes a short technical note on the theory behind the exercise. The final part of the book answers some questions about meditation theory and practice, points out alternative metaphysical assumptions that underlie meditation techniques, and offers suggestions on the pragmatic role of spirituality for the course of human evolution.

II. The Tool Kit

A. Tutorial

Tool Number 1: Getting Started

Silence is the great revelation.

LAO TZU

What constitutes a special meditation posture is a posture that allows for *stability with alertness.* Any posture that allows for that is valid. There is nothing magic about twisting yourself into a pretzel.

SHINZEN YOUNG[4]

AIM

This is a "getting your feet wet" kind of exercise. It's a tutorial to get you started right away without getting into the fine points. The only goal is to see for yourself what happens when you keep quiet for a few minutes. Spiritual technologies require no investment in equipment, or even in preliminary training. You have all the makings right now. You can always start from where you are and receive an immediate payoff.

PREPARE

The preliminaries for the practice of the techniques in this book involve time, place, posture, and attitude. They are the same for all the exercises. We will review them just once right here.

A TIME

Many people find that they can quite naturally carve out a half hour first thing in the morning, perhaps getting up a few minutes early. Others prefer a time before retiring to sleep. For others a midday walk alone for a quiet time is the way to go.

Time management is a matter of priorities. If you can find time for a coffee break, a superfluous phone call, a mindless TV program, you can find time for a meditation break. Even if you don't have time for the aforementioned time-wasters, you will find time for meditation, when you learn for yourself that it is a time-saver, rather than a time-waster. With a very brief time investment, you will gain a perspective on your self and life that will give you a sense of your life's priorities. You can open up hours of free time when false priorities are put aside.

A PLACE

Are there any "Do Not Disturb" places in your home? I suppose the bathroom is such a place, and could serve as a refuge of last resort. Retire to such a place, reassuring every-one that you will return alive and well in a half hour, but till then you are to be left alone. Maybe your only resort is to leave your place of work or house "on an errand," or go out and sit in your car.

If your phone is a tyrant, maybe you need a place away from your phone. Can you switch off the bell? Can you pretend you're not there? If you weren't around you wouldn't be an-swering the phone, and the world wouldn't come to an end. The best solution would be to hear the phone ringing as you remain undisturbed, aware that you are in charge of the phone, the phone is not in charge of you.

A POSTURE

Find a posture in which you can on the one hand be *stable, settled in,* and *still,* while on the other hand maintaining yourself *alert.* A posture that is relaxed, yet alert: that is the key.

Some people get attached to certain postures, like the full lotus position. Others, in reaction, are adamant against any special positions or postures at all, claiming that meditation can be part of any activity in any part of your daily life. No need to be dogmatic about either extreme. Experiment for yourself. What position helps your body be relaxed and stable, while maintaining your mind alert? In what posture can you best "settle in," but without dozing off to sleep?

Throughout the book, we will point out ways of integrating these spiritual techniques into your everyday activities. Aside from that, experiment with the best posture for you during the set-aside time you dedicate formally to these techniques. If the lotus position does it, fine. If you can lie on the floor or a firm surface without dozing off, that could be the answer. Or try sitting on a chair without slouching, back erect without being rigid, arms and legs uncrossed, hands on your lap, palms open.

TRAP

You can fool yourself in two ways. You can say, "I have to sit in a perfectly aligned posture in order to meditate." Or you can say, "I never have to sit in such a posture, because I meditate in everyday life."

ATTITUDE

This initial technique is an experiment with just being silent. It can reveal to you the immense amount of stuff that is going on when supposedly nothing is going on. There is no predetermined goal. Just be silent for ten minutes and see what happens. Be an observer. That's all you have to do. There is no good or bad result. Whatever happens is fine. Just be silent. Be a curious observer, and see what happens.

TECHNIQUE

1. Adopt a posture that allows you to be relaxed, yet alert.
2. Take several deep breaths as you begin to calm your body, compose your mind, and settle into this exercise.
3. Then just be still, and notice what's happening inside you.
4. If you catch your mind spinning a million miles away so that you forgot what you are doing, just say to yourself "Isn't that interesting!" and keep on observing.
5. If you catch your feelings and daydreams carrying you off again, just say, "There I go again," and keep observing.
6. Be still, and observe, until you are ready to end this exercise.

TECHNICAL REFERENCE

This is a rudimentary form of "Awareness" meditation, what Buddhists call *vipassana*. Awareness brings not only a tremendous healing power to the parts of you that are unwell. More importantly, the energy of your aware attention is a force for transformation of the parts of you that are well. You will be introduced to many ways of practicing this powerful technique. In addition to *vipassana* you will also be introduced to other kinds of spiritual techniques. The focus in the techniques remains on practice, rather than theory. However, at the end of the book you will find a typology to help you to classify the techniques, relate them to each other and determine the levels at which they operate.

ONE MINUTE MEDITATION

Spiritual awareness is more than a Sunday morning or early morning affair. You use your eyes all the time, not just for a half hour in the morning. It is no less important to keep your spiritual vision functional all day long. The techniques you practice at a special time and place need to be integrated into everyday life. Each technique in the book will end with a suggestion for integrating the exercise into the course of your daily activities. The One Minute Meditation and the Twenty Minute Meditation complement each other. Each is necessary for the vitality of the other.

Consider your day like a game of musical chairs. The music plays and you keep marching round and round. From time to time during the day, let the music stop. Just say to yourself, "Stop!" And then notice what your thoughts and feelings are. What's going on in you that you really weren't paying attention to?

B. Spiritual Awareness (*vipassana*) Techniques

1. Body Awareness

Tool Number 2: Body Attunement

I have visited in my wanderings shrines and other places of pilgrim-
age. But I have not seen another shrine blissful like my own body.

BUDDHIST TEXT[5]

Logic is in the eye of the logician.

GLORIA STEINEM

AIM

You will learn a simple yet powerful technique for focusing
your attention and energy on the present moment, on the
"now" of your life. You will move out of your head, out of the
past with its regrets, its feelings of guilt, its resentments, into
the present moment. You will move your head out of the future
with its fears, its anticipations, its dreams, its dreads, back into
the present moment. You will locate yourself fully in the only
place where your life happens, namely, in the experience of
yourself alive right now.

PREPARE

You will focus on *feeling* your bodily sensations. Note that
thinking is not *feeling*. This is the key to this technique. You are
not about to think of, analyze, or label the different parts of
your body. You are to experience the feelings and sensations in
each part. Thinking about "my heart" is one thing. Being

wordlessly aware of the pulsating beat is something else again. You will center on this simple present awareness without thoughts or words.

TIP

When you notice your mind spinning off into anticipation of what lies in store for you the rest of today or tomorrow, or rerunning yesterday's personal soap operas, note calmly what is happening, and then gently return to your present bodily feelings.

TIP

If you are uncomfortable with your eyes closed, keep them open, but lower your glance to a spot three or four feet in front of you. Keep your gaze relaxed and unfocused. From time to time experiment again with keeping your eyes closed. Discover what works best for you.

TRAP

To guide your awareness through the experience of this technique, the various bodily parts are named. Don't get caught into thinking about the parts like a doctor. Experience the feelings without the labels. Your "neck" doesn't know where the neck ends and the back and shoulders begin. Direct your attention to your precise feelings in that general area. Don't conduct a diagnosis.

TECHNIQUE

1. Adopt a relaxed alert posture. Take a deep breath to clear your mind and settle into a contemplative frame of mind and body.

2. Pay attention now to sensations and feelings in your body that you probably are not aware of at all. Methodically shift your attention to these feelings throughout your body, starting with the top of your head.

3. Notice first your scalp. Note the feeling of your hair on the top of your head. What sensations are you experiencing on the top of your head?

4. Now pay attention to your forehead. Experience any tension there. Note the temperature of the air against your forehead.

5. Focus now on the touch of your eyelids against your eyes.

6. Move your attention next to your nose, your tongue, your lips, your throat, your neck, the back of your neck.

7. Keep moving your conscious attention down through your body, your right shoulder, your left shoulder, your upper back, your lower back.

8. Notice the feeling of your clothes against your upper body, the sensations in your chest, your stomach, your lower abdomen.

9. Notice the weight pressing against your hips, your thighs, the sensations in your knees, the calves of your legs, the feeling of your feet inside your shoes, your hands on your lap.

10. Once again, move your attention through your body, this time more quickly, starting at the top of your head, and moving down to your forehead, your eyes, your nose, lips, tongue, throat, neck, shoulders, back, chest, stomach, hips, thighs, knees, ankles, feet, the soles of your feet.

11. Once again sweep your attention through your body, ending up with an awareness of the totality of sensations and feelings resonating through your body as a whole.

12. Now, without naming the parts, move your attention around your body, experiencing as lucidly as possible the feel-

ings in each place. If there is a place of numbness or lack of sensation, stop there and note carefully what you experience.

13. Continue for five more minutes or until you are ready to end the technique and return to ordinary consciousness.

TECHNICAL REFERENCE

The word "meditation" is used as a catch-all to refer to anything from relaxation and self-hypnosis to the highest reaches of mystical union with God. Our aim is to go beyond the psychological relaxation and tension-reduction by-products of the meditation process. Tension is the enemy of contemplation, but the spiritual technologies in this book are more than relaxation techniques. Like many of the techniques, this exercise in body awareness is deceptively simple. While your conscious attention is on your body, there is an unconscious impact on your spirit. More on this later.

For now, note this one caution. During this bodily awareness technique you can become very relaxed, and very drawn to rest in the stillness that comes over you. You can rest in this stillness and go into a trance. There is nothing wrong with this. It is a form of self-hypnosis and can be quite delightful. But this does *not* help sharpen your awareness. This does not advance the ability of your higher mind or spirit (more about this later) to open out to the divine presence. So the bottom line of the body-awareness technique is to keep your awareness active. Focus on the present feeling, the present sensation, the now. Don't seek to rest in relaxation for its own sake.

Finally, there may be times when stillness completely overwhelms you and you can hardly resist surrendering to it. In such a case you can profitably let go and surrender. A spiritual guide can be helpful here.

ONE MINUTE MEDITATION

(1) There is a place in life for words and plans and thinking and logic. There is also a place where these get in the way, the so-called "head trip." With its dreams and fears and prejudices, my head sweeps me away from the present moment and into the future, or it rushes me into the past with its guilts and regrets. At such times I need to summon myself back to the present moment where life and action exist. My misguided logic needs the antidote of love and intuition, feeling and sensing. When this happens, pause: begin to pay attention to your body and its feelings, as you did in this technique. Your body exists not in the past or the present, but now. Attention to your feelings is a sure-fire summons back to the present moment. In a nutshell: Question: "Where am I? I don't know whether I am coming or going." Answer: Check your body. "Here I am!"

(2) Bodily tension is a useful signal that I am out of tune with my life or with the people in my life. Bring this mini-technique to bear on the tension. Let yourself experience it, without labeling. The very act of noting it, accepting it, will tend to dissolve it. However, it's not just the tension that will disappear, but the body's resistance to the present troublesome situation will also disappear. There is no better way to get out of the head trip and into the present than following the lead of your bodily sensations.

Tool Number 3: Body Wisdom

Once the abandoned self in the body has been touched by listening and caring for it, the body awakens and acts like a partner to consciousness. The self in the body, the dreambody, becomes personal power, unfolds its wings, stretches beyond its imprisonment in doings, and acts out its dreams, its myths. One sees this happen in dreambody work, as individuals follow their bodies, let them flow freely and discover the myth behind personal life, the experience of freedom.

ARNOLD MINDELL[6]

Meditation, however, is anything but a cure-all and has dangers too. Many people use meditation as a method for relaxation and may complicate a problem that already exists: lack of extraverted involvement. For such people, the indiscriminate use of meditation may unnecessarily increase loneliness and contribute to reducing lively contact with reality.

ARNOLD MINDELL[7]

AIM

To pay caring and friendly attention to bodily sensations with special attention to those bodily signals that are often labeled negatively. Tension, pain, illness, hiccups, and goosebumps are bodily words. The body is the voicebox of the unconscious. Bodily sensations are the language of unconscious. To give the label "symptoms" to discomfort and tension is to invalidate these signals. Pain is your friendly messenger bringing you very important news about your life situation. The goal of this exercise is to magnify the voice of that friend so that you truly hear it, and so that it won't have to shout even louder to get your attention.

PREPARE

This is a bodily awareness exercise but done with an attitude of complete acceptance and love for your body and everything it is telling you. Your intention is not to make your pains go away. Let your attention to your body be respectful rather than manipulative. Adopt the attitude that your body knows best, not that "you" know best.

Hearing what the body is trying to tell you requires great patience and practice. Allow this exercise to go wherever it goes. Don't entertain preconceived ideas about its "success." What happens, happens.

This is not necessarily a "healing" exercise. Healing implies a "disease" or "defect" to be healed. Consider the possibility that the so-called disease could be the friend and the healer the enemy. A healing agenda can be a way of telling the body to shut up. Bodily disturbances are best not dismissed as pathological. They may well be the healthiest health-oriented messages you will ever hear. When you shut them up, you may well be forcing them to shout more loudly to get your attention.

TECHNIQUE

This technique will be carried out in several stages, starting with an exercise to get your body into a relaxed alert awareness mode.

1. Stand with your feet under you, relaxed, eyes open. You are very much present in the here and now. Feel the solid floor beneath you; focus on the solid floor.—See it with your feet.

Feel the solidness beneath you for miles and miles. Shift your attention to the top of your head.—Sense with your head the space between you and the ceiling to the infinite edge of the universe. Come back now to the room and notice the space around you—the forms, the colors, the people. Pay attention now to the sounds around you, the sounds outside. Now pay attention to the sounds inside you. Sense your heart beating.

2. Now become present fully—sounding the heart sound "HA." Now, "HA—EE," now "OOO . . ." as you sit down, relaxed and alert and close your eyes.

3. Take a deep breath and relax. Now turn your attention to your dominant hand, to your right hand if you are right-handed and to your left hand if you are left-handed. Allow a feeling of energy to build in your dominant hand. Continue to focus on your dominant hand. Imagine a dial controlling the intensity of your concentration. The highest reading is ten and you are now at four. As you turn the dial up your attention becomes greater, more intense, more concentrated on your dominant hand. Your concentration is now on 5, and 6 and 7 and 8 and 9 and now 10, the highest intensity of your concentration. Allow the energy to build from your conscious attention.

4. Now move your attention throughout your body, checking your sensations all through your body beginning with the top of your head. Notice first your scalp, the feeling of your hair on your head. Now pay attention to your forehead; experience any tension there. Focus now on your eyelids against your eyes, your nose, your tongue, your lips, your neck, the back of your neck, right shoulder, left shoulder, your back against the chair. Note the sensations in your chest, your breast, your stomach, your lower back, your hips, your genitals, your thighs, your knees, your calves, the feel of your feet in your shoes, your right arm, your left arm, your hands in your lap, and back to your dominant hand.

5. Now move your attention through your body at your own pace. Stop and pay attention to any place where there is special tension or discomfort or lack of ease. Focus on the sensation in this special place or places in your body. Hold your attention there. Hold.

6. Now become the sensation in that part of your body. Identify yourself with it. Amplify it. If it is tense, allow it to feel even more tense. If there is an ache, let the ache increase. You want to hear the body's message loud and clear. Amplify it; experience it clearly and unmistakably.

7. This sensation is your friend and it's telling you something. Now put some questions to it. It won't answer verbally. Perhaps when you question the sensation, some images will come to mind, and you'll have a feeling related to the sensation, or it will connect with something in your life, or you'll have an intuition.

Now get into the sensation and ask: Why are you feeling like this? What's your concern? What's on your mind? If I changed something in my life, would you change your tune?

8. Amplify the sensation again. And beware of images that come to mind or connections and feelings related to your life and experience. Amplify and have your radar out for the over-tones and what your body is telling you.

9. Again, direct your attention methodically to the sensa-tions throughout your body from head to toe, until again your attention is stopped by a special sensation that summons your detailed attention to the message your body is sending you.

10. When you are finished, take a deep breath, relax your focus and come back to ordinary consciousness and open your eyes.

TECHNICAL REFERENCE

The body's messages are absolutely vital information. Aware-ness is much more important than relaxation. To make a fetish

of relaxation to the detriment of awareness can be dangerous
and destructive. Be careful not to use meditation simply as a
relaxation technique. Tension is a signal just as a siren is a
signal. Block your ears to a siren and you will be at peace, but
you ignore the siren's message at your peril. Your body's signals
just are not divided into good and bad—they are all good because they are all you. What others may see as a defect, you best
see as a characteristic. Love, accept, and listen to your body and
it will be your friend and keep you on course to your personal
fulfillment.

ONE MINUTE MEDITATION

Make friends with your body—it has more to tell you every
moment about your health, your relationships, your needs,
your place, your effectiveness for success than your eyes or
your ears can tell you. Whenever a question enters your head,
tune in to your body and listen. For example, shall I have a
snack or cigarette? How am I tuned in to this phone call? Why
am I suddenly depressed? Am I ready to study? How far shall I
run today? Do I really want to go to bed with this person?

Tool Number 4: Absolute Stillness

The practice of quiet is an exercise . . . in surrender and willingness, a discipline of letting go. Each time we sit quietly, the silence takes us as far as we can go at that moment toward the loosening of the preconceived images of ourselves. . . . Yet . . . it is risky to view silence as a means to any kind of end. To shackle it with such expectations is to disrupt its natural quality from the outset and to enter instead into the confounding area of success and failure, of achievement and grasping.

GERALD MAY[8]

AIM

The goal is to let go of preconceptions and negativities that bind us. The preconceptions that bind us to the past, and the preconceptions that pull us away from the present and into the future, are the cause of our dissatisfaction. But it is dangerous to make the goal of ridding ourselves of these the goal of quiet sitting (*Zazen*). Such a goal itself can become a preconception and source of dissatisfaction. The well-worn ruts of such conscious expectations are precisely what we must let go of. The purpose of sitting is to sit, and that's enough.

PREPARE

Rule one in stillness meditation is to be still. You may become physically tense, no matter how comfortable your initial posture is. Don't move. Become aware of the tension. Note where it is and note every detail of how it feels. Don't try to *will* it to go away. This only gives it more power. Use your will to become completely aware of it. Stay with this awareness until the awareness dissolves the tension.

Your body is apt to protest against the stillness by developing aches and pains. Give these the same treatment: precise, keen, detailed, sharp awareness. So don't move your limbs or readjust your posture to ease the pain. Don't try to *will* the aches away. Just saturate them with your awareness.

Make a game of not moving. Be strong.

Consider this exciting possibility: you may for the first time in your life experience *pain without suffering*. Listen to Anthony de Mello who recounts how during a Buddhist retreat he experienced excruciating pain in his knees and back while in the lotus position:

> I decided not to fight it, not to run away from it, not to desire to alleviate it, but to become aware of it, to identify with it. I broke the pain sensation up into its component parts and I discovered, to my surprise, that it was composed of many sensations, not just one: there was an intense burning sensation, a pulling and tugging, a sharp, shooting sensation that merged every now and then . . . and a point which kept moving from one place to another. This point I identified as the *pain.* . . . As I kept up this awareness exercise I found I was bearing the pain quite well and even had some awareness left over for other sensations in other parts of my body. For the first time in my life I was experiencing pain without suffering.[9]

Until your body becomes accustomed to perfect stillness, it will protest. Use awareness on the pain. The reward is great. Your body will become still. You will experience the peacefulness that comes with this stillness.

Note, finally, that you will become aware of itching and pricking sensations, and the temptation to scratch will be great. Your awareness in the ordinary course of events is hardened and numb to such sensations. Don't scratch, but analyze the itching in loving detail. Be grateful for the challenge. Become aware of the amazing complexity of a simple itch. Don't try to *will* it away, but become extremely absorbed, curious, and identified with it until it disappears.

The reward of this exercise is a profound blissful stillness.

TIP

If you have the urge to cough or sneeze, let this too become the target of your awareness. Pretend you are in mortal danger from an enemy nearby, and you *must* not cough or sneeze. Rejoice in the power that your awareness and conscious attention give you.

TECHNIQUE

1. Adopt a relaxed yet alert posture. This is the posture you will maintain without movement through the duration of this exercise. Close your eyes, take a deep breath, and compose your body and mind.

2. Start to become aware of the sensations in your body in careful detail. Start with the feeling of the hair on the top of your head, and move down through your body to the very tips of your toes, and how they feel in your stockings and your shoes. Leave out no part of your body, starting now with the hair on the top of your head.

3. Notice every single sensation in every part of your body. If you come to a place that has no sensation at all, pause there for a few seconds; if no feeling emerges, then move on. A time will come when no part of your body will be numb or cut off

from your awareness, when you will be in touch with the lively sensations in every single part.

4. Keep moving slowly from head to foot, and then, once again, from the hair on the top of your head to the tips of your toes. Note the differences each time your attention moves through your body. You will pick up sensations that you did not pick up before. Though your posture is immobile, your body pulsates with change.

5. You will become aware of sensations which are very fine and very subtle, sensations that only a person in deep concentration and deep peace could possibly perceive.

6. Now let your awareness become attuned to your body as a whole. Feel your whole body vibrating with sensations of all different kinds. Stay with this for a while.

7. Now return to the awareness of your body part by part . . . then once again become attuned to your body as a whole.

8. Notice the deep stillness that has come over you. Note how completely still your body is. Stay aware of your body. Don't let surrender to the stillness cause you to lose the awareness.

9. It is important that you do not move at all any part of your body during this exercise. Each time you feel the urge to move or scratch or fidget, become aware of this urge. Don't act on the urge, but become as completely aware of it as you can. If a sound in the room disturbs you, pay sharp and close attention to the disturbance in yourself. Your conscious awareness will cause the urges and disturbances gradually to die away, and once again your mind will become as still as your body.

10. Alternate your attention: first to the sensations in your body part by part, then to your whole body vibrating with all types of sensations. Then notice the stillness.

11. First the parts, then the whole body, then the stillness. When you are finished slowly come back to ordinary conscious-

ness, open your eyes, and orient yourself by looking around
the room.

TECHNICAL REFERENCE

Zazen is the Japanese Buddhist word for "sitting meditation." *Zazen* is an end in itself, rather than a means to an end.
The practice of quiet sitting, of silence, of stillness, has been a
universal and absolute path to wisdom in every contemplative
tradition. It is the antithesis of the goal/action orientation of
western culture. If *Zazen* seems to you to be a "waste of time,"
you can at least look on it as an interesting experiment. As with
the other techniques, make it a working hypothesis, try it, test it
out for yourself.

All of our thoughts and images are inadequate to grasp or
understand God. God can be touched in stillness. Where God
can't be caught in words, God can touch our experience in
stillness. This is the first basic assumption behind this stillness
technique.

Secondly, this exercise is an antidote to the fundamental
cause of human unhappiness as diagnosed by Buddhism,
namely our misplaced desires and addictions. We turn away
from the present reality of our lives that is staring us right in the
face, and cling instead to what used to be, what might be, or
what we think should be. As a counterpoint and antidote, sitting
meditation brings us inexorably back to present reality. In sitting quietly, the rift between "is" and "ought" is overcome.
Absolutely quiet sitting simply cannot happen without absolute
acceptance of present reality—the reality of those simple rest-
less sensations revealed to awareness in our bodies as we sit in
stillness. It is acceptance of the now; it is letting go of all the
plans and goals and regrets clamoring for our attention and
conspiring to tear us away from present reality.

Finally, there is more to our lives than the subconscious and conscious streams of thoughts and feelings. We have a need to attune ourselves to a dimension that transcends ordinary consciousness, to the true person we are meant to be. When I open myself up in stillness to the touch of God, I am opening myself up to the highest possibilities of my own true nature. My everyday thinking puts me in touch with the world that I share with everyone else. Sitting quietly in contemplation puts me in touch with my unique potential and destiny which sets my life apart from the lives of everyone else.

ONE MINUTE MEDITATION

There are natural pauses in the day when you are in between jobs, when you are expecting someone to arrive or waiting for something to begin. Turn these moments into absolute stillness, relentlessly focusing your attention on your present sensations. With all the agenda of your daily life whirling in your mind, you sit quietly, absolutely still. The purpose of sitting quietly is to sit quietly. You acquire an attitude to extend to all your activities as you resume your daily tasks. As the purpose of your sitting is to sit, let the purpose of your eating be to eat, of your walking to walk, of your bathing to bathe, and of your sleeping to sleep.

2. Breath Awareness

Tool Number 5: A Breathing Game

The breath forms a bridge between the conscious and unconscious systems. By watching it, one can observe an unconscious function at work, learn to exclude interferences, and help self-regulating processes set in.[10]

AIM

You will experience one of the most ancient, most universally practiced, most powerful, and most rewarding techniques for sharpening your awareness. The technique is simplicity itself. The payoff is automatic and profound. To be blunt, this breathing game yields "the most bang for the buck" of any meditative practice you can undertake.

PREPARE

This is a variation on the techniques that direct your attention to bodily sensations. The sensation you focus on here is your breathing. Your breathing is what you will observe.

Breathing exercises take many forms. Some focus on a deliberate effort to control, deepen, and slow the breathing process. Not here, though. In this technique, concern yourself not with controlling the breathing process but with observing it. So don't try to breathe rhythmically, or deeply. Don't try at all. Let your breathing breathe you. Just let it be and observe it. Shallow breaths, deep breaths, irregular breathing, yawns, regular breathing, it doesn't matter. To help keep your focus, you will count your breaths. That's all. Just count.

TIP

Say to yourself the word "breathing" as you breathe in. Then count "one" as you breathe out. Then, again, "breathing" as you inhale, and "two" as you exhale, and so forth to the count of ten.

TIP

Make a game of it. Tell yourself, "I won't miss a single count for fifteen minutes."

TRAP

No matter what happens, stay with the count. Your mind says, "This is stupid!" No matter—just stay with the count. Your mind wanders; no matter—just start over again. You lose count, or keep counting over ten; no matter—just start again with the count of one.

TECHNIQUE

1. Here are the rules. Resolve to count every breath you take for the next fifteen minutes. Each time you exhale, count: first time, count "one," next breath, "two," then "three," and so forth up to "ten." Then start with "one" all over again. Starting at "one" again after you reach "ten" keeps you alert. It's *not* like counting sheep on and on till you fall asleep!

2. Start by closing your eyes, and taking three deep breaths to clear yourself and relax. Then note the sensations in your head, your neck, your chest, your shoulders and back, your thighs, your feet, your hands. When you have settled down,

composed and attuned, turn your attention to the sensation of your breathing.

3. Begin to count your breathing, from "one" to "ten" each time you exhale and then from "one" again.

4. Once or twice during the exercise you might check your brow and your eyelids: is there any tension? Observe it till it relaxes, then continue to count. This is not a high stress exercise. Just count. Even children count. This exercise yields powerful results, but your part is quite simple: just count.

5. If you keep losing the count, you might want to say the word "counting" as you breathe in, and then the number as you breathe out.

TECHNICAL REFERENCE

Breathing is a primal powerful metaphor. It signifies and manifests mind/body integration, self/environment harmony, and divine/human relationship. Attention to breathing brings awareness of harmony at every level of your being. It also reveals tension points where harmony is lacking.

Eastern mystics speak of *prana*, breath, the life-force of all existing things. Western tradition speaks of Spirit, the breath of God, creating and enlivening every single thing in the universe. Your breathing (spiritus/*prana*) is the physical manifestation of your spirit, that place in your being that touches the Divine Spirit. In this exercise you have just begun to appropriate the power of this *spirit*-ual force or *prana*.

ONE MINUTE MEDITATION

You can use your breathing to diagnose your inner state and condition. Consider. What do the following reveal about your inner spiritual climate? Arhythmic breathing? Shallow breathing? A gasp? Deep regular breathing from the diaphragm? A sudden holding of breath? A trembling long sigh? A deep relaxed sigh?

In other techniques you will see how adjusting your breathing can adjust your spiritual climate.

Tool Number 6: Breath Awareness (*vipassana*)

The more the air is cleansed of vapor, and the quieter and more simple it is, the more the sun illumines and warms it.

ST. JOHN OF THE CROSS[11]

Keep breathing.

SOPHIE TUCKER[12]

AIM

You will learn another method of breathing meditation. Whereas "The Breathing Game" approached breath as a mantra (the repetitive counting), now you will note your breathing in the spirit of "mindfulness," what the Buddhists call *vipassana*. A side-effect is the sense of calm and relaxation that results. This is not the aim, however. Alert, though relaxed, mindfulness is the aim.

PREPARE

You will be paying attention to the sensations in your body as you take air in and let air out. This exercise is moving you in the direction of the much more subtle type of awareness that characterizes divine contemplation. This is a simple but very refined technique. So you may notice that you seem to be more distracted than you were in the practice of other techniques. If you catch your mind wandering, just return to the awareness of your breathing sensations.

TIP

To be effective you should stay with the breathing awareness for twelve to fifteen minutes.

TIP

This is an awareness exercise, not a breathing exercise. So let your breathing be spontaneous, shallow or deep, irregular or not. Don't try to control it. Just notice it.

TRAP

Discouragement because your attention wanders is a trap. Know that the very fact you notice distractions means that your awareness is increasing. This is reason for encouragement. Don't judge yourself. Just return to the task.

TECHNIQUE

1. Close your eyes, and breathe deeply as you settle your mind and body into a relaxed alert attitude and posture.

2. Begin by making a leisurely survey of the exact sensations in each part of your body. Start with the sensations you feel at the top of your scalp and move slowly down your body to the soles of your feet in your stockings, and note, without labeling, the exact sensation in each part of your body at this particular moment of time.

3. Then shift your awareness to your breathing. Focus on the sensation in your nostrils. Notice the feeling of the air as it enters and leaves your nostrils. Don't follow the air into your

lungs. Keep focused on the air as it passes through your nostrils.

4. Resolve not to miss a single breath. Don't try to control your breathing. Just notice it. If your attention wanders, firmly and gently bring it back.

5. As you settle into this exercise, begin to notice the flow of air in the right nostril. Compare the feeling to the flow in your left nostril.

6. Notice the temperature of the air as it flows in; as it flows out; the sense of warmth and coolness on the left side as compared to the right side.

7. Stay with this awareness for about fifteen minutes.

TECHNICAL REFERENCE

Underneath the ordinary world of flux with its constantly changing thoughts, feelings and sensations lies a form of consciousness of a completely different kind. Here resides the deeper permanent self with its own rhythms and perspectives. Breathing awareness gives access to this self. The medieval mystic Tauler calls this place "the ground of the soul"; Meister Eckhart calls it "the little castle"; for Teresa of Avila it is "the inner castle," for John of the Cross it is "the house at rest in darkness and concealment," and for Catherine of Siena it is "the interior home of the heart." For all of these it is the place where the spirit touches the presence of God.

ONE MINUTE MEDITATION

Down through the centuries this exercise is highly recommended as a recourse in time of trouble. It brings peace. It brings self-control. And above all, it helps you maintain an inner joy in times of outer turmoil. Test this out in your own experience. Take a "*vipassana* time out" during you day. Your breathing is a friend and a support that you have with you always. You don't have to decide to breathe. You only have to decide to pay attention.

Tool Number 7: Breath Contemplation

> We ought not to have or let ourselves be satisfied with the God we
> have thought of, for when the thought slips the mind, that god slips
> with it.
>
> MEISTER ECKHART[13]

> I have sometimes wondered if mystics—or rather mystic aspirants
> —are not in quest of something which most people already have.
>
> RAYMOND SMULLYAN[14]

AIM

This contemplative exercise will help you to experience a
little more explicitly the religious dimension implicit in the
breathing techniques. It is an opening out to divine presence,
but with minimal use of concepts, images and words.

PREPARE

Breathing is a natural symbol of your relation to God, and
God's activity toward you. Spirit, which means "breath," is a
traditional name of God. This breath awareness technique ad-
verts explicitly to this divine imagery. You will use your breath
as a language to communicate with God. During this technique,
as you breathe out, you will express your feelings toward God
(for an everyday example, think of how expressive a sigh of
weariness or a sigh of longing can be). And your "breathing in"
will be a metaphor for receiving divine love and support (as an
everyday example, think of how you throw open a window to

fresh air, and breathe in renewed strength and relaxation). Such "breathing communication" with God, though wordless, can be very real.

TIP

Keep the focus on your breathing and associated feelings. Let the divine reality be a kind of wordless environment in which the breathing communication takes place.

TRAP

If the "God imagery" inspires words or negative feelings, just observe these without evaluation, gently let go, and focus on the breathing.

TECHNIQUE

1. Posture your body to be relaxed and alert. Breathe deeply to ready your mind for contemplation.

2. Direct your attention throughout your body, noting the feelings and sensations in each part. Especially direct your awareness to those places where you feel pain, or tension, or numbness, or itchiness. Let the energy of your conscious attention flow into those places where your body is distressed or is without feeling.

3. Now come to the awareness of your breathing, as the air flows into your nostrils and flows out. Stay with the awareness of these breathing sensations for a few moments.

4. Breathe in peace . . . Breathe out tension . . .
   Breathe in calmness . . . Breathe out anxiety . . .

5. Be aware that the air that you breathe is energized by the power and presence of God. Breathe in this Spirit, this presence . . . Breathe in the power, this energy.

6. Be aware of the air that surrounds you as an immense

ocean bathed in God's presence and God's being. As you draw the air deep into your lungs, you are drawing in the presence and being of God. With each breath that you are drawing in, consider that you are drawing God in.

7. Breathe God in . . . Breathe out anxiety . . .
   Breathe God in . . . Breathe out darkness . . .
   Breathe love in . . . Breathe out fear . . .
   Breathe in divine energy . . . Breathe out all impurity . . .

8. Stay with this awareness.

9. See your whole body becoming radiant and alive through this life-giving Spirit you are breathing in. Breathe in life and light . . . Breathe out darkness. . . .

10. Stay with this awareness until you are ready to end the exercise and return to ordinary consciousness.

TECHNICAL REFERENCE

Much of what passes for prayer stays at the level of a "head trip." Often prayers seem to take the form of issuing orders to the Divinity: "make it rain"; "cure my headache"; "get me this job"; "help me lose weight." This breathing technique takes you out of your head and places your whole being in God's presence, allowing you to realize that your whole being is filled with God's being. It invites faith in the divine life of grace within you, and trust in God's initiative, rather than the human initiatives that characterize the head trip. It short-circuits conscious effort to manipulate God through words, and opens direct access to the ever-present divine reality.

ONE MINUTE MEDITATION

Your breath can serve as an instant hot line to God when you are depressed, frustrated, empty, idle, or just have a moment to tune in. No need to put your problem in words, or to formulate any requests, or to express particular feelings, or to diagnose your difficulty. Just lower your eyes, take a deep breath, and immerse yourself in the air that surrounds you, air charged with the presence of God. This Spirit knows better than you the prayer you need to express. No words are required. Breathe in divine life and energy, breathe out darkness and confusion. The Spirit, the breath of God knows what you require. The Spirit is not waiting for your orders, but for your readiness to receive.

Tool Number 8: Breath Realization (*anapana-sati*)

Your breathing is your greatest friend. Return to it in all your troubles and you will find comfort and guidance.[15]

Many things that start off easily end in misery. Meditation starts with difficulty and ends in pleasure, bliss, harmony.

BERNARD GUNTHER[16]

AIM

Awareness of breathing brings awareness of the present moment. Awareness of the present brings aware action. Aware action is full freedom.

PREPARE

Attend to your breathing. This technique preferred by the Buddha, and central to every mystical tradition, will center your attention and your energy in the present moment.

Having practiced other breathing techniques, you are invited here to make a greater time commitment, to stay with this technique for an extended period (but no more than an hour).

Again, this is not breath control but breath attention. If you follow your breathing the control will take care of itself. The very act of attending to your breath as it goes in and out of your nostrils will bring changes. Without any effort on your part, your breathing will slow down from sixteen to eighteen times per minute to perhaps half of that. It will become more rhythmical. And as you watch it, you will see your breathing become more abdominal, just as effortlessly as you slip over into abdominal breathing when you fall asleep. Here, of course, we are talking about aware breathing, not sleepy breathing.

And again, note that this is not a breathing exercise so much as an awareness exercise. Breath is an ideal object for *vipassana* concentration. A shoplifter can concentrate on the ideal moment for snatching a sweater and escaping. An alcoholic can concentrate mightily on how to sneak an extra drink. Such concentration is no good. It is born of craving, of fear, of ignorance. But you cannot crave, or run away from, or be deluded by, your breathing. The moments when you are focused on your breathing are moments of supreme detachment, freedom, and presence to the ever real, ever changing here and now.

TIP

Notice the air as it enters and leaves the nostrils. Note how cool or warm it is as it goes in and goes out. Note how each breathing differs from the one before. Note the differences in the feeling of your right nostril and your left nostril as you inhale, and again as you exhale. The infinite subtleties of your breathing will fine-tune the subtlety of your awareness.

TRAP

Do not follow the air as it goes into your lungs. Just note the passage through your nostrils. This will keep your attention finely focused.

TRAP

It may be easier for you to slip into mantra meditation by saying the word "in" as you breathe in, and "out" as you breathe out. The word will substitute for breath as the object of concentration. However, your concentration will be sharper, purer and more subtle if you don't do this, but maintain your attention on the breathing itself.

TECHNIQUE

1. Assume your meditation posture and for at least twenty to thirty minutes, but no more than one hour, pay attention to your respiration, in all its subtleties, in great detail, but without any attempts to control it.

2. When your attention wanders, calmly note this, and gently direct it back to your breathing. When an outside sound distracts you, note the reverberations it causes inside you, and then gently return to your breathing.

3. Wandering attention is an occasion for awareness but not for self-condemnation. When you note you've been distracted, say "How interesting," not "How awful."

TECHNICAL REFERENCE

1. Breathing is a metaphor for the interface between you the individual, and everything else. Attention to breath makes it experientially clear that you are indeed not an individual cut off from the world. As through a swinging door you breathe in sustenance from the world and release it, transformed, back to whence it came. Breath, *Spiritus*, is a primal name of God (in Christian belief the third person of the Trinity). The attention paid to physical breath or *spiritus* in this exercise touches your spirit at the deepest part of your being. Awareness of breathing draws you into a nameless place where the Spirit touches your spirit. This is the source of the abiding power in every mystical tradition of breathing meditation.

2. There are spiritual writers like William Johnston[17] who want to distinguish "breathing for human potential" from "breathing with faith." Do you need a "pious" intention to reap the benefits of breath-awareness? I suggest that a pious patina or overlay is not required. Let the intention be simply to do the exercise, without ulterior motives or goals. The results are in the doing. God is perfectly capable of acting without our cheerleading. What the Spirit may choose to accomplish is not our problem. What is under our control is to pay attention to the air going in and the air going out of our nostrils. That's enough. As with the other techniques, check this out with your own experience.

Related to this distinction is the Buddhist concern to distinguish *samadhi* from *vipassana*. The concentration and mind control produced during the exercise you just did is *samadhi*. Such concentration is artificial compared to real life. It is difficult to sustain when the exercise is over. To put life at the service of meditation is a reversal of priorities. *Samadhi* is not an end in itself. It is to be at the service of life. It is a training exercise for *vipassana*, a responsive awareness occurring at the heart of action, any action, from driving in a traffic jam to taking a shower.

3. The eastern arts of karate, judo, and tea ceremony witness the intimate link between breath control and performance. Western culture has adopted breathing techniques for singers, athletes, and mothers giving birth. Breath control has resulted in more remarkable claims from the power of levitating or becoming invisible to more verifiable feats of slowing/stopping the breath or the beating of the heart for unusual periods of time. All mystical traditions warn against getting sidetracked by such singular and peculiar novelties. They have nothing whatsoever to do with spiritual or personal mastery, or personal

growth. To direct effort and attention to such aberrations is to miss the point altogether.

ONE MINUTE MEDITATION

Your breathing is your greatest friend.

Return to it in all your troubles and you will find comfort and guidance.[18]

1. Your breath is there for you whenever you need a pause or a refresher. First, just interrupt your action, or stop your train of thought/feeling. Tell yourself, "STOP!"

2. Take a deep breath, and relax.

3. For one minute, just observe your breathing in and breathing out.

4. Now, focused and energized, you are ready to give your attention to the matter at hand, but now without fear, without craving, without your customary illusions.

3. Mind Awareness

Tool Number 9: Inner Watching

"I have heard of a doctrine of enlightenment. What is its method?"

"We walk, we eat, we wash ourselves, we sit down."

"What is there that is special in these actions? Everyone walks, eats, washes themselves, sits down. . . ."

"Sir, there is a difference. When we walk we are aware of the fact that we walk; when we eat, we are aware of the fact that we eat, and so on. When others eat, walk, wash themselves, or sit down, they are not aware of what they do."

THE BUDDHA

"What's on your mind, if you will allow the overstatement?"

FRED ALLEN

AIM

You will learn to increase your self-awareness and power of concentration in two ways. First, you will increase your control over your thoughts by observing them rather than by trying to dominate them. Second, you will become very aware of the subconscious tapes that your mind plays for you all the time underneath your ordinary level of awareness.

This technique works by indirection. You cannot control your thoughts directly. If I tell you "Don't think of an elephant," of course you can't help but think of an elephant. But if I invite you to watch yourself thinking of an elephant, this is something you can do. And if you watch yourself thinking about

50

the elephant, the thought of the elephant will cheerfully go away without any effort on your part.

This is a simple but infallibly effective technique for dealing with the distractions that stand in the way of concentration and contemplation.

PREPARE

See yourself as setting up an observation post to watch the train of your thoughts and feelings as they pass by. Here is the key: realize that there is a difference between watching the train go by, or getting on the train of thought and being carried away. You want to watch the train, not get on it. A switchman, if he watches a train, can control it, but if he hops aboard, the train controls him. He will be carried off on whatever track the train takes. So like an outside observer, watch the train of your thoughts; don't get aboard.

TIP

It might help to imagine the darkness in front of your closed eyes as a screen on which your thoughts will pass.

TRAP

There is no such thing as a bad or inappropriate thought. However "terrible" the thoughts and feelings, you, the observer, just note, "How interesting," and quietly let it go.

TIP

If you find you have unwittingly jumped aboard a train of thought, no harm done. Just get off, and begin again to watch the train.

TECHNIQUE

1. Uncross your arms and legs, straighten your spine, close your eyes, take a deep breath and relax.

2. Turn your attention to your dominant hand, your right hand, if you are right-handed, otherwise to your left hand. Allow a feeling of energy to build in your dominant hand. Continue to focus on your dominant hand.

3. Imagine a dial controlling the intensity of your concentration. The highest reading is ten, and you are now at four. As you turn the dial up, your attention becomes greater, more intense, more concentrated on your dominant hand. Your concentration moves to five, then six, seven, eight, nine, and finally to ten, the highest intensity of your concentration.

4. The sensation you feel in your hand is caused by your conscious attention. Again, allow the energy to build for thirty seconds. Now take a deep breath, relax, and begin to observe your thoughts.

5. For the next few minutes, be silent and watch your thoughts go by. Don't follow them. Just observe.

6. If your mind goes blank, just wait for a thought to appear, and observe.

7. You can say to yourself "I am thinking, thinking . . ." to keep your attention on your passing thoughts.

8. When you end this technique, while it is still fresh, immediately write down the patterns of thought you observed, and how they made you feel.

TECHNICAL REFERENCE

In this exercise, you have taken a first step toward harnessing the power of your subconscious mind. The subconscious is that part of your mind that operates below the level of your normal everyday awareness. It is constantly sending you messages, most of which you are not aware of. There is a direct connection between those messages, and what is going on in your life. You are invited, for now, to accept this connection as a working hypothesis, to be tested out for yourself. In other techniques you will be checking this hypothesis with your experience.

ONE MINUTE MEDITATION

From time to time through the day, stop. Notice what thoughts are running through your head, especially when the thoughts and feelings have nothing to do with what's going on in your life at the moment. Ask yourself: "If I had my choice, would I choose and rejoice in the scenario my thoughts are presenting to me?" We will see in other techniques that you *do* have a choice.

Tool Number 10: Counting Your Thoughts

Nothing is worth grasping because nothing lasts. So as much as we grasp and hold the body and sense, the feeling, the memory, ideas, reactions, and observation, so much do we make a separate "self," and so much do we suffer through this attachment.[19]

No self, no problem!

HINA TYANA DHAMMALOKA

You can't stop the waves, but you can learn to surf.

SWAMI SATCHIDANANDA

AIM

Without judging or evaluating, you will note the unstoppable flow of your thoughts and feelings. You will see what a waste of energy is the effort to staunch this flow. The flow of thoughts and feelings reflects the flow of your life. Fear and desire cause you to try to hang on to what you have, and keep you from gently surrendering to the flow. In surrendering to the flow of thoughts, you will sense the freedom that comes from surrendering to the flow of your life's moments, without attachment and clinging. Freedom from attachment leaves your energies free to respond and live.

PREPARE

This exercise is a deep practice of meditation. You will prepare by composing the body, quieting the breath with your attention. With your mind thus concentrated, you will set up an "observation post." The rule is simple. For ten minutes, you will count your thoughts. You are like a traffic commissioner counting the flow of vehicles on a busy street. Some of the vehicles are trucks, some are cars, some are bicycles. You don't judge, you just count. The trucks are loud, the bikes don't make a sound. You don't care. You just count. Traffic comes in spurts; for a moment there is nothing, and then a whole long line. You just count. So with your thoughts. Just observe and count. Some thoughts and feelings will sneak up on you; others will try to grab you. You stay calm. You just observe and count.

TIP

As your concentration grows, your awareness will be powerful enough to keep you from getting caught up in the contents of the thoughts and feelings. You are just an observer of the mind traffic; all you want is an accurate count.

TRAP

Some cars are new and flashy; others are clunkers that shouldn't be on the road. That's no concern of yours. So with your thoughts. Angry thoughts, guilty feelings, encouraging visions, discouraging memories, it's all the same to you the observer. You're just counting. No labels, no judgments, no evaluations.

TIP

A passing cyclist might engage you in conversation, or a motorist might ask you directions. You're distracted from the count. When you note you've been distracted, just wave goodbye and pick up where you left off. If you have a bad feeling about being distracted, just count that feeling too. It's not bad for you. You just count here.

PROCEED

1. Adopt your relaxed alert meditative posture. Note the sensations in your body, with special attention to where there is discomfort, and to where you are numb and without feeling.

2. When your body is settled, become very aware of your breathing in and breathing out for a couple of minutes, until your breathing, too, is settled.

3. Now let your mind be like a screen that you are going to watch. Set up your observation post and start to count your thoughts as they appear. You may have word thoughts, and picture thoughts, and feelings and sensations associated with them. You are very alert. You don't let anything sneak by unnoticed. You are so absorbed in a careful count that you don't have time to worry about the content of your thoughts and feelings. Bad or good, very weak and subtle, or very strong and overwhelming, coming in a rush or coming few and far between, it's all the same to you. You are just carefully counting.

4. You might get a thought like: "Why am I doing this?" No problem. Just count it, and wait for the next. You might get distracted and lose count. No problem. Just pick up where you left off. If you can't remember, then resume with the last number that you can remember.

5. Continue this exercise for ten minutes.

TECHNICAL REFERENCE

Most people will count twenty-five to fifty thoughts, even one hundred or more. You will notice whether you have more picture thoughts or words. You will have noticed the cycles and repetitions of patterns.

Above all, you will sense the liberation that comes from realizing that you are not these thoughts and feelings. Your attention gives you power over them. They can't sweep you away.

And when temporarily they caught you up, you were able to gently release yourself and return to the observation post. These needs, desires, angers, delights, guilts, don't own you. You own them. And you can watch them with interest, and let them go.

Note that there is a deeper point to be made here. As the keenness of your observation increases, you become more sensitively aware of the variety of components and vibrations that make up each thought and feeling and sensation. The solid content and power of these thoughts and desires that used to seem so powerful and overwhelming are seen to be fragile, momentary, and ever-changing. You are freed from them not because you "should" be detached, but because you see them for the poor, weak, ever-changing phenomena that they are. They are empty. This is the *nada*, the nirvana, the nothingness at the heart of Buddhism, which is supremely liberating, which frees you to live each moment without grasping it or holding on to it for dear life. You let go of it for dear life. You get a glimpse of the doctrine so baffling to non-Buddhists, a glimpse of the fullness of liberation that lies at the heart of nothingness.

Nirvana is not something to aim at. Nor is there any profit in measuring your progress or degree of liberation. It is enough to do the exercise and let the chips fall where they may. To desire *nirvana* is an attachment. It's a Catch-22. Humble and proud of it. You only get it when you don't want it.

ONE MINUTE MEDITATION

When your mind's in a whirl, or when you are about to face a stress situation, pause. Let your body and your breathing settle for a moment. Then set up a mini-observation post. Notice with great care just what's going on inside you. Your attitude: "There I go again: how interesting." This is a pause that will really free you up.

4. Sound Awareness

Tool Number 11: The Sounds of Mantras

How often have I sat down at out-of-tune pianos . . . and winced at the first notes as I pressed the keys; nevertheless . . . I have found that from the moment I started to enjoy the music my ear started to correct the inaccuracies. My listeners, too, as they adjusted themselves inwardly to these out-of-tune sounds, experienced this odd phenomenon, with all the intervals suddenly seeming to be in tune.

PETER MICHAEL HAMEL[20]

AIM

You will learn that every sound can be a mantra to focus your attention and awareness. You will learn to *observe* sounds rather than labeling them "annoying" or "beautiful" or "harsh" or "soothing." You will experience the silence at the heart of every sound.

You will let go of ideas like "your most favorite sound" or your "least favorite sound." A sound is just a sound.

For the space of the exercise, however, forget all aims. Just let the sounds speak to you.

PREPARE

Some people are visualizers. When you talk to them, they answer, "I see what you mean." Other people are listeners. When you speak, they answer, "I hear you." This exercise is for them. It focuses on sounds. Visualizers, too, may be surprised at all the sounds they've never paid attention to before.

Begin this exercise by blocking your eyes with your fingers and plugging your ears with your thumbs. Listen to your body's life-sounds, your breathing, the circulation of your blood.

TIP

Make a game of picking up every little sound and vibration. See if you can hear subtle sounds, distant or near, that you never noticed before.

TRAP

You might find yourself getting annoyed or even angry at someone sniffling or coughing, or tapping a foot, or clicking a ballpoint pen, or be disturbed at a radiator banging. Just notice your annoyance, like an outside observer. Don't condemn your annoyance or analyze it; just note it—"How interesting"—and resume your attention to the sounds.

PROCEED

1. Begin as noted above by covering your eyes and plugging your ears with your hands. Listen to the sound of your breathing for ten full breaths. Then gently put your hands on your lap, palms open, and keep your eyes closed.

2. Now pay attention to the sounds all around you. Listen closely to every single sound, to every nuance of every sound. Note as many sounds as possible, loud and soft, near and far.

3. At first you will tend to identify and label where the sounds are coming from, what they are. That's fine. Identify as many sound sources as possible.

4. Then begin to attend to the sounds without identifying them. Listen as you would to an orchestra or a rock group. You hear the total effect without identifying the individual instruments and voices. You are in the midst of an orchestra of sound.

5. Without identifying the origin of the sounds, note the subtle textures. One sound is often made up of many other sounds. Pay attention to the variations in pitch and intensity. How many nuances can you notice?

6. Floating as you are in an ocean of sound, your body becomes very still, and your spirit opens up. Notice your connectedness to this vast ocean of sound. Notice what you feel. Then return to the world of sound.

7. You are a listening post to this universe of sound. Again, note your feelings as you listen. Do you feel stillness, love, a sense of being part of a harmony? Then return to the world of sound.

8. Alternate between the sounds themselves and the sense of harmony you feel with them. Back and forth. Two sides to a single harmony.

9. Know that God's power underlies and sustains each sound. It is the divine harmony sounding around you. Listen to the divine symphony.

10. Rest in this world of sound.

11. Rest in God.

TECHNICAL REFERENCE

A mantra is a sound that occupies the mind, thereby opening the spirit to divine contact. There are many ways of occupying, slowing down the mind, even making it blank, so that the quiet and empty space offers no barrier to God's unspeakable, unimaginable presence. Attention to sound is like attention to breathing, attention to bodily sensations, attention to an image. It can serve the purpose of quieting the mind, thereby releasing and unfolding the spirit to God's presence. No need to pay $450 to have the Transcendental Meditation Society assign you a mantra. The sounding world around you produces for you a mantra without end twenty-four hours a day, if only you choose to pay attention.

ONE MINUTE MEDITATION

Music is sound. Noise is sound. People, machines, the natural environment make sound. Any time, morning, noon or night, pause a moment to refresh yourself. Stop, take a deep breath, then quietly listen. There is no sound that cannot be a mantra. Noisy people keeping you awake can become a divine lullaby singing you to sleep.

Tool Number 12: Devotional Mantra

There is a time to keep silence and a time to speak.

ECCL 3:7

Popular forms of meditation are most likely . . . no more useful than repeating the word "money" over and over again for relaxation.[21]

AIM

The goal is to quiet the mind, thereby releasing the spirit for experiential contact with God or Transcendent Reality. You will learn to use a sacred word or phrase to focus the mind so that God can step in and lift your spirit. It is a technique that clears the mind that in the absence of its accustomed clutter, your spirit can respond to God's initiative.

PREPARE

Choose a mantra, a sacred word or phrase. Eventually you will want to stay with one (or possibly two) as your very own for permanent use. For now, choose a favorite name of God, such as Peace, Love, Shalom, Compassion, or a favorite short invocation of God, such as "Lord, have mercy," *"Namu Amida Butsu," "Hare Krishna," "Aum Mane Padme Hum."* Even a meaningless phrase will do. It's not what the mantra is that counts, but what the mantra does.

The technique comprises four steps: (1) a prayer of faith in God's presence and of petition for God's help; (2) three deep

breaths to relax and move you to your center; (3) twenty minutes of centering mantra-focused contemplation; (4) the Our
Father or some other standard ritual prayer to help move you
back to normal consciousness.

TECHNIQUE

1. Recall that God is present at your deepest self. It is to this
divine presence at what the mystics call "the fine point of the
soul" that mantra meditation directs you. For about one minute, recall this presence as God's help in the centering exercise.

2. Close your eyes and take three deep breaths, each time
filling your lungs with air and then slowly exhaling, forcing all
the air from your lungs before you take another deep breath.
As you exhale, know that you are moving down from your head
to your "center," your heart, down from your head to your
spirit where God contacts self.

3. Now say your mantra. Then be still.

4. When you notice any idea, image or thought, very gently
repeat your mantra.

5. The rhythm of the prayer goes like this: mantra–pause–
blank–thought–mantra–pause–blank–thought–mantra.

6. The blank pauses may be longer or shorter. It doesn't
matter. Each time you are aware of a thought or image, gently
return to the mantra.

7. Continue for twenty minutes.

TIP

Instead of using the mantra as a "thought-stopper," you
might find it more profitable to simply repeat it rhythmically
synchronized with your breathing.

8. When you are ready to finish, repeat a psalm or the Our
Father or a similar vocal prayer.

9. Open your eyes, stretch, and look around to orient yourself.

TECHNICAL REFERENCE

Like many other contemplation/meditation techniques, this exercise has benefits on many levels. Psychologically, there is calming of anxiety and release of the physical tension and stress associated with it. The mantra exercise under the rubric of TM or "transcendental meditation" is often offered at this level.

"Centering prayer" uses the same mantra technique as does TM, but its intent is religious, viz. a direct immediate wordless contact with God. The effects of this encounter are experienced and explained on a religious level. The love and peace and renewed strength from this prayer are experienced as gifts from contact with the indwelling Spirit.

At both levels, experience is primary. Explanation, theory and works are secondary. Are TM and centering prayer identical at the level of experience, but distinct at the level of explanation? Or is the former a totally non-religious exercise as opposed to centering prayer which is religious? If the impact of the meditator's intention is stressed, you'll see the exercises as essentially different. If, on the other hand, you stress God's ability to touch humans regardless of human intent, you will play down the differences of TM and centering prayer as they impact on the meditator. To use a traditional theological distinction, the former answer sees the technique as working *ex opere operantis*. The latter answer sees the technique's effectiveness as *ex opere operato*.

I incline toward the *ex opere operato* view. Just do the technique, and let the results and explanations take care of themselves. God is perfectly capable of touching the soul, whether or not you dress up your exercise in religious clothing.

Tool Number 13: Mantra Contemplation

The devotional *mantras* such as the Lord's Prayer and the Amida Buddha prayer are, perhaps, the easiest for religiously minded people to accept wholeheartedly. But this type of *mantra* leaves a film of religious attachment covering pure awareness.

MARION MOUNTAIN[22]

As long as we perform our works in order to go to heaven, we are simply on the wrong track. And until we learn to work without a why or wherefore, we have not learned to work, or to live, or why.

MEISTER ECKHART[23]

AIM

This is a mantra technique from a Zen perspective. Here it is less appropriate than ever to speak of a goal. The exercise will point you to pure awareness in the "now" of your experience. The exercise leads you to gently let go of any attachment that would draw you away from the present moment. Such attachments can come in the guise of a "worthy" goal, like "having a good meditation" or "being detached and present in the 'now'" or "becoming one with God." Paradoxically, the goal of being united with God can get in the way of being united with God; the goal of having a good meditation can get in the way of having a good meditation; the goal of becoming detached is itself an attachment, is itself a failure to be detached. So doing the technique is sufficient. As for results, just let it be.

PREPARE

Choose a mantra. It is better if the mantra is not emotively biased toward either good feelings or bad. The mantra should not tend to hook you into any train of thought or emotional pattern. A mantra like "Lord, have mercy" might be all right, but it *could* lead you to dwell on your past sinfulness and draw your consciousness into a climate of guilt. A mantra like "Peace and love" might be all right, but it could make you attached and anxious to feel good and peaceful. A sacred mantra like *Namu Amida Butsu* ("Praise to the Compassionate Buddha") or "Our Father who art in heaven" might be all right, but it could lead you to be attached to your own holiness.

Counting your breaths from one to ten and then starting over again is an example of a safe, emotively neutral mantra. The neutrality of even this mantra could be spoiled if you made it into some kind of competitive game with yourself, criticizing yourself when you lose count, and congratulating yourself when you don't.

TIP

Choose for your mantra a nonsense phrase or expression. Try "bah–nah–nah" ["banana"?] or "oh–pee–ee–see" [OPEC]. More commonly, people choose a mantra in a language foreign to them. "Aum Mane Padme Hum" is Sanskrit; "Kyrie Eleison" is Greek; "Namu Amida Butsu" is Pali; "Domine, Mecum" is Latin. Though these phrases qualify as "sacred," their unfamiliar language can remove the emotional bias.

Another possibility is to say "breathing in" as you inhale, and "breathing out" as you exhale. The poet Alfred Tennyson used to repeat his own name. You could do that for your mantra, or repeat some other melodic name from history or from literature like, Omar Khayyam, for example. If phrases like these or nonsense phrases make you uncomfortable, then don't use them. The mantra you choose should be neutral and comfortable. It should not draw attention to itself one way or the other.

TECHNIQUE

Adopting your regular relaxed alert posture, you will silently repeat or chant the mantra. How often should you repeat it? You have two alternatives. Use the mantra either on a (1) rhythmical or on a (2) as needed basis.

(1) At first, rhythmic repetition of the mantra is the easiest and most effective approach. Find a comfortable rhythm. You can synchronize it with your breathing. Or you can let the rhythm of the mantra's syllables carry you along, much like a musical phrase in a song that plays in your mind.

(2) The second approach uses the mantra in the fashion of an eraser head on a tape recorder or the "delete" button on a computer. When you are totally centered with your spirit opened up to experience in the present, your thoughts are still, your mind is empty—a blank. But you will notice your thoughts and feelings starting up again. When this happens, quietly hear the mantra in your mind. Paying attention to your mantra is a gentle way of letting go of the habitual patterns that tie you up mentally and emotionally. You repeat the mantra on cue. Let the appearance of stray thoughts and feelings trigger the mantra. Distractions become a cue for return to the mantra, return to the still point of present awareness.

1. Begin by closing your eyes and taking three deep breaths. Count five as you breathe in, hold for five, and count five as you exhale, forcing all the air out of your lungs. Do this three times.

2. Now for a few moments pay attention to all the sounds

that you hear around you. Note the quality of every single sound, loud and soft, distant and near. Listen to the world of sound around you.

3. Gently begin to repeat your mantra. Find your own rhythm for the silent reciting or chanting of the mantra. Thoughts and feelings will come into your awareness. Note them quietly and objectively as you would glance at a flock of birds flying by in the sky outside your window, and return to the mantra.

4. The mantra is your base. The mantra anchors you to your center. Stay with your mantra.

5. When you are ready to end the exercise, this Zen story can be your transition to ordinary consciousness.

In her search for Zen, Stacia went to a Japanese monastery where she spent several months. Continually, she asked the Zen Master, "What is Zen?" and received no answer.

To show how humble she was, she cleaned the communal bathrooms. The Zen Master was not impressed and she felt humiliated.

When Stacia realized that if she wanted to clean bathrooms, she could do that anywhere, she decided to leave. She told the Zen Master of her decision. He replied, "That is Zen."[24]

TECHNICAL REFERENCE

"God is not religious," says the Catholic southern novelist Walker Percy in *The Moviegoer*. Zen practice reflects this spirit. What is present is neither sacred nor profane. It just is. Each "now" is the fullness of reality for our experience. It is diminished only by what pulls us away from it.

ONE MINUTE MEDITATION

Let your mantra be your friend. When you see yourself unfocused and ineffective in your ordinary life, let the gentle
repetition of the mantra bring you back to the present point of
most power in your life which is *right now.*

5. Awareness in Action

Tool Number 14: Karma Yoga

Not everyone is able to meditate profoundly, regularly, consistently. Everyone, however, is able to practice what is known in India as karma yoga, the yoga of action. . . . The karma-yogin or yogini continues to get up in the morning, eat breakfast, go to work, interact with people during the day, spend time with the family, read, listen to music, make love, and sleep . . . but with a subtle yet significant difference. . . . All these actions . . . are opportunities to cultivate quiet awareness and the force of love.

GEORG FEUERSTEIN[25]

Just as the pure and polished mirror is completely transparent, receiving everything into itself without distortion and reflecting all objects as if they were appearing in it for the first time, so the enlightened mind is completely receptive and filled with wonder, seeing everything as for the first time.

WILLIAM JOHNSTON[26]

AIM

You will practice mindfulness outside of the usual meditation setting. For a short space of time, you will cultivate awareness in the midst of everyday actions as a rehearsal for bringing this attitude into the whole course of your life.

PREPARE

You will center yourself before you embark on this experiment. Let this experiment last thirty minutes. Set a definite starting time and ending time for the exercise.

TECHNIQUE

1. Begin by centering yourself, using one of your favorite "one minute meditation" techniques.

2. For the next thirty minutes, stay aware of your bodily sensations as you walk, and of your breathing as you move.

3. When some object (a cigarette, a television), or activity (sipping coffee, reading a book), or person (a passing acquaintance, a phone call for business or romance) engages your attention, be totally immersed in the "now" of that experience. Attuned to yourself, you are attuned to the other. Such a mindful attitude is expressed in the following two Zen texts:

> "Look at that person over there standing on the hill. I wonder what she is doing. Probably waiting for someone."
> "No, seems more like she's looking for something."
> "No, I'm sure she's waiting for someone. Let's ask her."
> "Excuse me. Would you tell us what you're doing here?"
> "Sure. I'm just standing on this hill."

> When eating, just eat, when walking just walk, when sleeping just sleep, and above all don't wobble.

4. Here are the ground rules for this technique:

(a) If you usually meditate in a group, for the next thirty minutes either be alone, or engage yourself with people who are not part of your meditation group.

(b) For the duration of this exercise, anything goes, provided you keep yourself centered and mindful, whatever you choose to do.

(c) Look at your watch to determine the exact time you are beginning and ending this exercise, and observe this time limit.

5. Get yourself centered, and then begin.

TECHNICAL REFERENCE

In the Christian mystical tradition, Ignatius of Loyola called such mindful living "contemplation in action." In Hindu tradition it is *karma yoga,* the path of action.

Life is more than a social or economic adventure, or an exercise in biological survival. The enlightened person, externally, seems to do pretty much the same things that everyone else does. Like everyone else, the enlightened person is occupied with money, sex, and health. Occupied, but not preoccupied. The quality of the experiences is different.

Mindfulness transforms ordinary activities into occasions for self-transcendence. Individual moments of time take on an eternal quality. Each moment has a value in itself, is self-validating. No ulterior motives are required or present. The mindful person acts not to be thanked, to please others, to make an impression, to be rewarded; rather the act itself is the reward. It's the difference between enjoying an apple rather than eating a low calorie dessert, between helping a blind person cross the street rather than doing a good deed, between satisfaction in a job well done rather than scoring points.

Mel was a truly enlightened Zennist. He was throwing a party one evening. Conversation turned to the single earring Mel was accustomed to wear on his left ear. John suggested that sailors wear an earring to signify that they had crossed the equator.

Eric speculated that such an earring could signal a spiritual crossing of a personal equator into a new hemisphere of one's life.

Eric suggested that the left ear could symbolize the freedom of one who stands to the left against conformity and conventions.

Sally pointed out that the left is associated with the occult.

Then someone asked Mel why he wore the earring on his left ear.

"I like to sleep on my right ear," he replied.

ONE MINUTE MEDITATION

This technique is less a spiritual exercise than it is a short rehearsal for enlightened living. The outcome of *karma yoga* is that all the moments of your life take on the quality of "one minute meditations." Until you are so transformed, the rehearsals remain useful. Coffee breaks and bathroom breaks can be opportune occasions for practice.

C. Fantasy Tools

1. Spiritual Techniques
—for Acceptance and Love

Tool Number 15: Love of Self

The sub-conscious mind plays a very important part in the interior life, even though it remains behind the scenes. Just as a good play depends on the scene, the lighting and all the rest, so too our interior life owes much of its character to the setting and lighting and background and atmosphere which are provided, without any deliberate action of our own, by our subconscious mind.

THOMAS MERTON[27]

AIM

You will take a first step toward controlling the subconscious backdrop of your spiritual life. You will learn a powerful technique for transforming the negatives in your life into positives, and for clearing your mind and feelings as you prepare to meditate.

PREPARE

This is a visualization technique. You will be projecting a scenario from your life story onto an imaginary movie screen. In this theater, you will be the projectionist; you are also the audience, the observer. But be as objective and emotionally uninvolved as a movie critic when you watch this movie. You will see events on the screen that the main character considers bad. But because you are objective, you will be able to see the good in these happenings.

TIP

A hint on posture. Arrange your hands and your feet differently depending on whether you meditate alone or in a group. In a group, you will want to be open to the energy and support of your fellow mediators. So keep your hands open, resting on your thighs, facing up. Keep your feet flat on the floor, comfortably apart, ensuring that your lower body is open and receptive to the surrounding energy.

When you are meditating alone, your concern is to conserve your meditative energy. Arrange your body so as to form a kind of closed energy loop. Rest one hand on top of the other on your lap, and cross your legs at the ankles. Your posture thereby signals that you are recirculating, not dissipating, concentrative energy.

TECHNIQUE

1. Close your eyes and settle your mind and heart by taking several deep breaths to relax.

2. When you are ready, imagine that you are standing in front of an elevator. The door opens and you enter. The door closes, and the floor indicator shows that you are on the tenth story. The elevator begins slowly to descend. You relax more and more deeply as the elevator slowly descends past the 9th floor, the 8th, 7th, 6th, 5th, 4th, 3rd, 2nd, 1st, and finally to the basement where it stops, and the door opens out to a small dimly lit theater.

3. You take a comfortable seat in front of the screen, and the movie begins.

4. Begin to project on the screen your life for the past twenty-four hours. Start with one of your mealtimes yesterday, with breakfast perhaps, or lunch, and observe scene after scene everything that happens.

5. When you see what seems to be a negative occurrence,

freeze the screen. Do an instant replay in slow motion. Observe the image on the screen carefully.

6. Remember that you, the movie critic, are not trapped in negative attitudes. You can notice other vibrations and feelings in the situation that the character on the screen did not notice. Don't analyze. Don't get "rational." Don't censor anything. Observe all the nuances. Feel the *wholeness* of the scene.

7. Let this be your principle: "Whenever a problem is born, the solution to that problem is created at the same time." As you gaze at the screen, see the solution appear in the problem . . .

8. Move beyond your initial negative judgment. See the wholeness of your life, the good and the bad. When you are ready, let the guilt, the regret, the "bad trips" you lay on yourself dissolve.

9. Forgive yourself. Acknowledge what you have learned.

10. And let the movie continue.

TECHNICAL REFERENCE

This technique assumes that there is a higher wisdom at the center of events in our lives. To limit our lives and our judgments by our petty labels about what is good and what is bad, what is useful and what not, what is logical and what stupid, what is attractive and what ugly, is to choose a very narrow life indeed. There is a place beyond good and bad where opposites are reconciled, where that higher wisdom is allowed to operate. This exercise is a way of getting in touch with that higher wisdom. The "bad" stuff in my life is the result of my resistance to this wisdom. The more I resist the problem, the more power I give to the problem. To stop resisting the problem is to see it as a signal from this higher wisdom, as an opportunity from this higher wisdom.

ONE MINUTE MEDITATION

When a negative feeling comes over you during the day, or when you have just come out of a negative situation, pause. Get in touch with the scene without prejudice and without censoring. Trust that the solution appears in the problem. Observe the solution being born as your feelings gradually transform under the calm energy of your objective attention. Suggested attitude: "I don't take this problem personally. Now let's see how I can learn what I need to learn from it."

Tool Number 16: Love of Enemy

> But I say to you that hear, love your enemies, do good to those that hate you, bless those who curse you, pray for those who abuse you.
>
> JESUS (LK 6:27)

> It is easier to forgive an enemy than to forgive a friend.
>
> WILLIAM BLAKE[28]

AIM

You will learn a technique for healing the hurt, the resentment, the psychological destructiveness you have suffered at the hands of someone who has deeply wounded and betrayed you.

PREPARE

This exercise is devotional. It is religious or at least humanist in orientation. It assumes that you belong to a family of humankind, a family from which not even your "enemies" are excluded. It assumes that humanity forms one family because at the root of each members being lies the spark of divinity, of divine life. Different religions name this indwelling divinity in different ways, "the buddha nature," "Brahman," "Christ." Or you can bypass these names altogether and use the image of light. Christ said, "I am the light of the world." Light is a universal symbol of the Godhead. On the one hand you will be visualizing the indwelling divine life. And on the other, you will

be visualizing one definite individual person in your life who is
causing your pain and resentment and hurt.

TRAP

This can be a very painful exercise if you are carrying around
a raw and open personal wound. There is a temptation to block
out the full force of negative feelings. The technique will work
best if you allow yourself to feel all the anger and all the hurt.

TECHNIQUE

1. Close your eyes, and assume a posture that is relaxed and
alert. Compose your mind, and then start to pay attention to
your breathing.

2. Breathe in peace . . . Breathe out tension . . .
     Breathe in relaxation . . . Breathe out anxiety . . .
     Breathe in light . . . Breathe out darkness . . .

3. Now direct your attention to a spot right in the center of
your chest. Here, right at the center of your being near your
heart, visualize a small glowing ball of white light. Assume that
this light is the being and presence of God (of Christ).

TIP

If it is comfortable for you, you could imagine Jesus' bodily
presence within you standing on a glowing white cloud dressed
in a flowing white robe, or just visualize the divine presence in a
small glowing ball of white light—whatever works best for you.

4. Feel the warmth and compassion of that presence. Feel
the love glowing from that presence.

5. Now visualize rays of gleaming light radiating from the
heart of this divine presence within you. Slowly let that radiating light grow brighter and brighter. Let this divine light begin
to grow and fill your body.

6. Notice that bright radiating white light moving downward into your abdomen and upward into your lungs and heart. Notice the light of divine presence growing even brighter as it streams up through your neck and into your head. Notice the light radiating and filling your arms and legs, and experience your whole body radiating with the light of divine presence.

7. Rest for a moment with the feeling of your whole body bathed and glowing with the bright light of God's presence.

8. Now see the light gradually diminishing, slowly drawing back to the center of your being, that spot in the middle of your chest near your heart. Know that the radiant light of God's (Christ's) presence is always there. This light never leaves you, never ceases to glow.

9. Now call to mind the person who has hurt you deeply, the person who is poisoning your feelings and your life. Picture this person as vividly as you can. Spare no detail at all. Visualize this person exactly the way she or he is. Take your time to experience this hurtful person and all the attendant pain.

10. Now notice right at the center of that person's being, right near his or her heart, a glowing ball of white light. See that light as the being and presence of God (of Christ) in that person's heart. That person might not be aware of it, but *you* see the circle of divine light radiating from the center of that person's being. The light and presence of God glows in your heart as the light and presence of God shines in the heart of that person.

11. Now see the rays from your heart extending outward in a clear bright beam, until the beam makes contact with the light in that person.

12. Hold that contact. Hold . . . Hold that contact . . . Hold until you feel something like a surge of current passing between you and that other person . . .

13. Then let go. Give thanks to God. When you are ready, bring this technique to an end.

TECHNICAL REFERENCE

This is not a universal humanitarian kind of love, e.g. for the anonymous starving people of Nigeria. This is not an abstract love that neatly bypasses the demanding relative, the treacherous friend, the jealous co-worker I live with every day. Nor is this a sentimental love, e.g. a feeling of union with birds and nature and all living things, to the neglect of that abrasive person who knows how to go for my jugular.

This is love based on will and choice more than feeling. The test case of humanistic love, of Christian love, is love of your personal "enemy," not the enemy in general, not "the communists," but love for that individual real person in your life who pains and hurts and destroys you.

It is not a feel-good kind of love, but a do-good. Are you ready, as appropriate, to do good for that person, or at least to will them no harm? So important is this that the founder of Christianity put it at the very center of his teaching:

A new commandment I give to you, that you love one another; *even as I have loved you, you must also love one another.* By this will all know that you are my disciples, if you have love for one another (John 13:34ff).

ONE MINUTE MEDITATION

When you see your problem person in ordinary life, be ready to recreate that transmission of light between the divinity within you and the divinity within him or her.

Tool Number 17: Acceptance of Life

When Banzan was walking through a market, he overheard a conversation between a butcher and his customer.

"Give me the best piece of meat you have," said the customer.

"Everything in my shop is the best," replied the butcher. "You cannot find here any piece of meat that is not the best."

At these words, Banzan became enlightened.[29]

The present moment is significant, not as the bridge between past and future, but by reason of its contents, contents which can fill our emptiness and become ours, if we are capable of receiving them.

DAG HAMMARSKJOLD[30]

AIM

This visualization technique is an opportunity to initiate a healing process in yourself through compassionate awareness and acceptance.

PREPARE

You will do three kinds of visualization in this technique, as you watch, observe, accept. You will be invited to visualize some thing or some person whom you love to think about, daydream about, and who makes you feel good all over; you will also be invited to visualize some person or some thing which you like to avoid. Finally, you will be invited to consider your life as a code language which speaks to you in situations and events, which are trying to tell you something.

TECHNIQUE

1. Close your eyes; take a deep breath to relax and attune yourself. Take a moment to bring your mind, your body, and your spirit into harmony and focus.

2. Now think of some thing, some event or some person in your life that you just love to imagine and that you are very grateful for. It could be a love in your life, a sense of well-being you have, something beautiful you like to imagine, a wonderful thing that happened to you. Vividly recreate this in your imagination. Savor it, enjoy it; think of what it gives to you. Imagine that this thing or situation is a language that is telling you something. What do you learn from it? Notice how your body feels when you are in this mood of acceptance.

3. Next, imagine some thing or situation or person that you would like to avoid in your life. Recreate it in your imagination. Pay very special attention to your reactions as they arise in response to this. Watch your reactions as they come forth. Don't try to stop them.

4. Notice the techniques of avoidance that you use, the techniques of non-acceptance that you use when faced with this negative in your life. See how your organism switches into the avoidance mode. Like a computer you switch on a non-acceptance program.

5. Notice how this program works at the level of your body. How does it impact on your feeling? on your mind? Notice all

your typical avoidance reactions. You have an avoidance style of your very own. What is it?

6. Now imagine that this situation is a language. It is life's way of trying to tell you something. Consider this situation and your reactions. What message does it have for you? What is it trying to tell you?

7. Return once again to that wonderful thing, or person, or event that you started out with. Visualize and enjoy it once again. Notice carefully all your reactions of acceptance. When you have your typical acceptance-program running, notice how your body responds—your feelings . . . your mind . . . Note your favorite style of accepting and enjoying things.

8. Now keep this acceptance program activated, and switch back to that unpleasant situation you visualized a moment ago. Accept it as a temporary fact of life. Don't run; don't avoid. Just allow yourself to watch it, to accept it as a fact. The same universe or God that speaks to you in pleasant words or events speaks to you also in these other words and events. Be at peace. Be still. Allow yourself to listen to God in all the events of your life.

9. Be still for a moment in God's presence.

TECHNICAL REFERENCE

For the religious person, especially in the Judaeo-Christian tradition, this technique is more than a working hypothesis. The faith hypothesis is that at heart, the universe is a loving place. You are loved unconditionally, no ifs, ands, or buts. The events in your life are loving messages. Accept these messages with interest and compassion. The positives and so-called negatives are gifts/grace. Healing is gift/grace. The only requirement is that you be still, attentive and allow it to happen.

ONE MINUTE MEDITATION

Every person you meet, every situation you get into, you can interpret positively as an interesting and informative message life has for you. Decode events. Ask what they are telling you.

Notice your avoidance patterns. Say to yourself, "There I go again." Break the pattern: take a deep breath and listen to what life is telling you.

Tool Number 18: Acceptance of Death

It has often seemed to me that our life on earth is like a swallow that suddenly darts into a brightly lighted banquet hall on a stormy night, lingers a moment, and then darts out a window at the other side. It comes from the wintry darkness into the warmth and light, and for a moment we see it clearly. Then it disappears again into the darkness outside.

That is how my life appears to me. I do not know from where I came into this world or where I am going; all I know is a brief span of light which I fly through all too swiftly. If your new religion can tell me why I am here and what lies before and after me, then I for one will follow it with all my heart.

COUNSELLOR OF KING EDWIN,
Bede's Ecclesiastical History of England

AIM

Through a simple visualization exercise, you will consider the value and meaning of your life as a whole. Through a consideration of your mortality, you will enhance your appreciation for the gift of your life.

PREPARE

This is a difficult exercise for many people in American culture. Many people live in a state of denial about their own death. Many have unresolved feelings about experiences of death in their own families. Get clear about the point of considering death. It is not to depress you. It is not to trigger a

89

psychological downer. This technique is offered completely and totally in the service of life. When you know your treasure is not in infinite supply, what you have is all the more precious. Someone has said that nothing clarifies your thinking so much as having a loaded gun pointed at your head.

TIP

Recall a time when you awakened from a nightmare, and how good and grateful you felt to be alive, awake, and well. Remember a time when you have emerged from an ordeal or had a terrible brush with danger, and emerged grateful and filled with resolve that your life from then on would be different. Take this exercise in that spirit, looking forward to a positive upbeat outcome.

TECHNIQUE

1. Close your eyes. Take a deep breath and relax. Take a couple of moments with the technique of your choice to bring your mind, your body, and your spirit into harmony and focus.

2. Imagine that you haven't been feeling at all well recently and you went to the doctor last week for a series of tests. Today is the day you are going to find out the results. It could well be that the tests will reveal a very serious illness. See yourself on the way to the doctor's office. Notice what you are feeling.

3. You have reached the office and are sitting in the waiting room. Note the pictures on the wall. What magazines are there to read? Are there other people in the room? Take a good look at them; notice the colors in the room, the rug, the furniture, the lighting. What are you feeling as you wait for your name to be called.

4. Finally your name is called; feel how you feel as you enter

the office. See yourself greeting the doctor. Notice the furnishings in the office. Is it bright or dim? Carefully look at the doctor, what the doctor is wearing, the expression on the doctor's face as you are invited to sit down. What kind of person is the doctor?

5. When you ask about the tests, the doctor starts to beat about the bush, seems to be hiding something. How does this make you feel? You tell the doctor that you want to be spoken to clearly and frankly and openly. The doctor gives you a long compassionate look. With eyes filled with sympathy, the doctor begins to explain to you that you have an incurable disease. You ask if it is terminal and how long you have to live. The doctor tells you that you can lead an active life during this summer, but that in the fall you will have to be in bed, and that you will not see another Christmas. What is your response?

6. Notice what you are feeling. Stay with these feelings . . . You leave the doctor's office and start walking home. You need some time to be alone with your thoughts. Notice your thoughts and feeling as you walk. Notice the other people in the street. How do you feel about them as you walk with this news in your heart? What is the weather like as you walk along? How does this make you feel?

7. You notice that you are wandering aimlessly. You have to decide where you want to go. What do you decide to do? Is there a particular person you'd like to talk to? What are you going to do and whom are you going to see the rest of the day?

8. Consider exactly whom you are going to tell the news to, and whom you will leave in the dark. Consider the plans you have made for the next few months. What are you going to do about work? About vacation? About upcoming important events in your family's life? How are you going to change these plans? See yourself making the calls, writing the letters, and

talking to the people you need to, in order to get all this orga-
nized. How do you feel about these next few months?

9. It is three weeks from now. You're at a party. Do people
know about you? How do you feel being in their company?

10. It's late at night. You go to bed, but you can't sleep.
Your thoughts turn to God. What questions would you put to
God? What dreams do you have that will have to be revised?
What unfinished business in your life now will you have to deal
with?

11. As you rest in God's presence, what feelings come to
you? Stay with this presence for a few moments.

TECHNICAL REFERENCE

Techniques like this one are perhaps more necessary in
urban America which so effectively insulates people from the
reality of death. Compare this to India, for example, where
death, funerals and cremations are part of the landscape day
and night. People who die are wrapped in a sheet, carried on
bamboo poles to the riverfront, and cremated at the river bank.
The fire takes seventy-two hours to burn itself out. Funeral
pyres burn incessantly. Death there is a fact of life.

Awareness of mortality can bring a perspective, urgency, and
richness to the limited precious moments of life, and foster a
special care for relationships and priorities.

ONE MINUTE MEDITATION

Every moment, every loss, every sacrifice, every change,
every choice is a small death a small letting go, and a dress
rehearsal for the main death. But the flip side of these deaths is

life. A physical loss can entail a personal gain, a choice not made is in support of a commitment that was made. And each religion in its own way defines the moment of death as the moment of rebirth.

Those not favored with religious faith can take hope from the testimony of the cycle of death and rebirth in nature. Or they can just wait and see.

1. Spiritual Techniques
—for Inner Wisdom

Tool Number 19: Your Inner Teacher

When the gods decided to create the universe, they made the heavens and the earth, the fishes, the trees, and the birds of the air, the animals, and, finally, human beings. Then they made Truth. They discussed among themselves where they might hide the Truth so that humans might not find it right away. The search for Truth was to be an adventure for human beings.

"Let's hide it among the stars," said one of the gods.

"No, let's put it on the far side of the moon," said another.

"They'll have a hard time finding it, if we put it in the ocean's depths," said a third.

Finally spoke the wisest of all the gods. "We will hide the Truth inside the deep mind and heart of human beings. They will search the world and universe to find the Truth only to realize finally that it dwells inside themselves and has dwelt there all along."

FERRUCCI[21]

AIM

You will access a transcendent level of awareness that goes beyond your usual assumed limitations, and therefore a dimension of your mind that usually goes untapped. This has been called your higher self, your deeper self, your inner wisdom. This technique addresses this dimension as your inner teacher.

PREPARE

There are many ways of putting yourself in touch with this level of consciousness, including both verbal and non-verbal

95

techniques. Here we will use a time-tested visualization exercise, and will address this level of mind verbally.

Prepare two questions to ask your higher self. Let these be questions that require more than a yes or no answer. You want a somewhat extended communication. Secondly, don't ask an emotionally loaded question like, "When will I die?" The answer will only be confusing, misleading, and untrustworthy, since loaded feelings only get in the way of the kind of atmosphere of quiet listening required for your higher wisdom to reveal itself. Problem-solving advice-type questions are good to practice with. Try questions that seek insights about friends, jobs, relationships, prospects, and plans. Stay away from questions that look for predictions about the future. This is practice. Keep it simple. Don't create pressure for the answer to be right.

Now write down the two questions you will address to your inner teacher.

TIP

Keep pen and paper at hand, for you will be writing down the answers you receive to these questions.

TIP

As for the answers, note the following:

(1) The answer will appear automatically; write down whatever comes at the moment without judging it.

(2) Write down the words as they occur, without waiting for a full thought.

(3) Don't be concerned where the thoughts are coming from; for now, be content to think that they come from another level of your mind.

(4) If you draw a blank, pause; allow yourself to think; write down these thoughts.

(5) If nonsense comes to you, write that down; if you think, "I'm not getting anything," write that down.

(6) Allow yourself to relax and enjoy this technique.

(7) If you keep a record of these answers and evaluate them objectively from time to time, you will learn a lot about your ability to relate to this inner wisdom you carry about with you.

TECHNIQUE

1. Close your eyes, and take two minutes to use your favorite technique to compose your body and focus your mind.

2. Imagine now that it is a bright refreshing spring morning. The sky is blue. The air is clean. You are in a field near the edge of a forest. Flowers and grass surround you. You are bathed and caressed by the breezes carrying the meadow's fragrances. Be aware of your feet on the ground, the clothes you are wearing, and the feeling in your heart. You feel ready and focused. There is a sense of expectation in your heart.

3. You notice now a path leading you into the woods. You find yourself easily walking along that path and into the woods. As you walk along notice the looks and the feels and the smells of the forest.

4. Ahead of you, you notice that the path is heading toward a clearing. You walk toward the clearing. You come into the clearing. You notice a schoolhouse in the clearing. Notice the walkway leading to the steps and door into the schoolhouse. You approach the schoolhouse and enter into the room inside. Your teacher is in front of the room and is expecting you. Walk up toward your teacher, up to the front of the room. Sit in the front desk in the first row facing your teacher.

5. Your teacher and you look at each other. Feel a close rapport with your teacher. Remember, your teacher represents

your higher self. Feel warmth and love and closeness between you and your teacher as you establish a deep rapport in feeling between you and your teacher.

6. Now ask your first question. Hear the answer, open your eyes, and write down the answer that you get. Then close your eyes again.

(If you are not writing, I assume you have no thoughts in your mind; allow yourself to think, and write these thoughts down.)

7. See now your teacher raising an arm so that the palm of the teacher's hand is facing you. See a ball of white light, bright like a small sun being created in the palm of the teacher's hand. Visualize another ball of bright white light being created at the center of your being, wherever that is for you.

8. Now a ray of light beams out from your teacher's palm and connects with the ball of light at the center of your being. Hold that connection between you and your teacher. Hold that connection between these two points of light. Hold.

9. Now ask your second question. Write down your answer.

10. Then close your eyes again, and continue to concentrate on your rapport with your teacher.

11. Ask your teacher now for a sign of how you can recognize when you are in touch. This could be a visual image, a smell, a taste, a sound, any sign that will indicate that you are in touch with your higher self.

12. Take a deep breath, relax your focus and at your own pace come back to ordinary consciousness and open your eyes.

TECHNICAL REFERENCE

If your experience is a downer, you hooked into some bad figure in your past, not your teacher. Joy is a sure sign that you made contact with your inner wisdom. Only indirectly is it God.

Directly it is access to a more intuitive, less assumption-bound level of your mind. You are touching a level of truth that often remains hidden in your mind.

ONE MINUTE MEDITATION

When you are perplexed, and your conscious mind is getting nowhere, use the sign you received from your inner teacher to access your own best intuitive wisdom about the best course for you.

Tool Number 20: Your True Nature and Purpose

"The object of meditation is to realize the one divine life pervading all things. The whole process is like filling a sieve with water." Having given his instruction, the Zen Master bowed and left.

His disciples pondered on the image of the sieve without getting any solution which satisfied them all. Some thought he was telling them that people like themselves in the world could expect only a temporary upliftment; some thought he was just laughing at them. Some thought he was telling them there was something fundamentally wrong with their ideas. Others thought that he might have been referring to something in the classics that he expected them to know.

In the end, the whole thing dropped away from all of them except for one woman, who made up her mind to see the master.

He gave her a sieve and a cup and they went to the nearby seashore where they stood on a rock with the waves breaking round them.

"Show me how you will fill the sieve with water," he said.

She bent down, held the sieve in one hand, and scooped the water into it with a cup. It barely appeared at the bottom of the sieve, and then was gone. "It's just like that with spiritual practice, too," he said, "while one stands on the rock of I-ness and tries to ladle the divine realization into it. That's not the way to fill the sieve with water or the self with divine life."

He took the sieve from her hand and threw it far out into the sea, where it floated momentarily, and then sank.

"Now it's full: of water," he said, "and it will remain so. That's the way to fill it with water, and it's the way to do spiritual practice.

It's not ladling little cupfuls of divine life into the individuality, but throwing the individuality far out into the sea of divine life."

TREVOR LEGGETT[32]

AIM

Your spirit is the name of that dimension of the Self where self touches God. It is the mystic's "fine point of the soul." Contained in that dimension is a sense of your true destiny, nature and purpose. The goal of this exercise is to consciously tune into your true nature. You feel frustrated and unfulfilled when the course of your conscious life and decisions is out of tune with your true destiny. You may not be able to articulate it verbally, but the perception resides there. It supports your life if you are in harmony, and gives warning signals of emptiness and unfulfillment when you frustrate it. So now you will tune in tangibly, though perhaps non-verbally, to your true destiny.

This awareness of your destiny serves to attune, unify and focus all your powers and all your energies. It is a profound act that orients your life as a whole when you are attuned to your true nature, when your life in all its details flows more spontaneously and more freely and successfully. When you are so attuned, your spirit attracts and harmonizes the energies of your conscious and your subconscious mind.

PREPARE

This is a visualization technique in which through the image of light you will evoke your awareness of God's presence, the awareness of your spirit bathed, immersed in and totally penetrated by the light of God's Spirit and life. A starting point might be the words of Jesus, "I am the truth and the light." Immersed in this light your will ask for an awareness of your truth, of your true nature, destiny and purpose. When like a compass your whole being turns in the direction for which it was made, then all the dimensions of your existence can become attuned to this true nature and support with their energies your destiny and purpose.

TECHNIQUE

1. Close your eyes, take a deep breath and relax. Take a couple of moments with your favorite technique to bring your mind, your body, and your spirit into harmony and focus.

2. Pay attention to your breathing in and breathing out. Breathe in peace, breathe out tensions; breathe in relaxation, breathe out anxiety; breathe in light, breathe out darkness.

3. Next, direct your attention to a spot right in the center of your chest. Here right at the center of your being, near your heart, visualize a small glowing ball of white light. Assume that this light is the being and presence of God. Feel the warmth and compassion of that presence. Feel the love glowing from that presence.

4. Visualize rays of gleaming light radiating from the heart of this divine presence within you. Slowly let that radiating light grow brighter and brighter. Let this divine light begin to grow and fill your body. Note that bright radiating white light moving downward into your abdomen and upward into your lungs and heart. Notice the light of divine presence growing even brighter as it streams up through your neck and into your head. Notice the light radiating and filling your arms and legs and your whole body radiating with the presence of God.

5. Rest for a moment in the feeling of your whole body bathed and glowing with the bright light of God's presence.

Intensify your awareness of this divine presence. Imagine that there is a dial that can dial the intensity of your awareness. The highest number on the dial is 10, and you are now at 4. As you turn up the dial see the light of God's presence becoming whiter, brighter and more intense. Now the dial is turned up to 5, to 6, to 7 to 8 to 9 and finally to 10, God's presence like the brightest sun you can imagine.

6. You are a channel for this divine light—your whole being opened up completely; you allow it to pour through you unresisting. See this bright light surrounding your body, completely filling the whole room.

7. At this point you are totally open and attuned to this light of God's presence. Allow yourself to be open and receptive to perceiving your true nature and purpose. Allow yourself to understand your destiny, wordlessly and intuitively perhaps, but you will become attuned to your true nature.

8. To receive this communication, put the question to God: "What is my own true nature and purpose?" Ask the question and pause to receive awareness of the answer in your heart.

9. Allow this sense of your destiny to grow and penetrate throughout your whole body and being. Allow the vibration of this true nature of yours to penetrate every level of your existence, the levels you know and the levels you don't know about.

10. Now begin to imagine that your true nature and destiny is completely satisfied—that you are attuned to your purpose and that is accomplished in you in every corner of your being.

11. Notice again the brightness of God's presence flowing into every corner of your being. Whatever pockets of darkness or shadows exist, let them be dissolved by the brightness and intensity of the light of God's presence.

12. Let this light draw back now to the center of your being. Know that the light of God's presence never leaves you, always dwells at the heart and center of your Spirit.

TECHNICAL REFERENCE

Your life is guided in part by your conscious choices. It is directed also by the sets of assumptions and belief systems that operate subconsciously, those self-fulfilling prophecy tapes by which your inner self-image plays itself out in public. This exercise directs you to a third source of guidance that operates at a "super-conscious" level. It has many names: higher wisdom, divine guidance, inner spirit, voice of intuition. It is an elusive voice, often unheard, more often unheeded. We carry inside us more information than we commonly use.

Many feel more comfortable relating to this inner divine guidance in the concrete and personal form of an inner guide. Such an inner advisor symbolizes and mediates the guidance we are talking about. It functions as a friendly ally that makes accessible to you the invaluable store of unconscious wisdom you possess. Guides take different forms for different people. Some picture Christ as walking with them, others the Buddha. For still others, a guardian angel is their constant guide, or a beloved spouse or parent who has died and now lives with God. There may be as many identities for the inner guide as there are people. But whatever the guide's name or form or appearance, it mediates and makes accessible to you the inner divine wisdom which is your birthright.

Accept these observations with an open mind and a large grain of salt. Assume an inner guide as a working hypothesis, and test its value in your own life. You need not believe in a metaphysical world populated by angels, guides, or divine incarnations. Beliefs are for using, not for believing. God's voice can reach the open heart, whatever name is assigned to that voice. So be open, and see what happens.

Consulting an inner guide is a surprisingly common practice, and with a long history.

ONE MINUTE MEDITATION

The philosopher Soren Kierkegaard said that the greatest mistake we can make is to speak of God as if God were absent. Oblivious as we are, the fact remains that we live in the ocean of divine presence. From the divine end, the hot line is always open. You just have to pick up the phone on your end. Talk directly or use the guide, whichever works best.

Tool Number 21: The Flowering of the Rose

One speck of dust contains the whole earth; when one flower opens, the whole world comes into being.

HAIKU[33]

Like a young plant hitherto quietly and intermittently developing which suddenly begins to breathe harder and to grow, as though in a miraculous hour it has become aware of the law which shapes it and begins to strive toward the fulfillment of its being, the boy, touched by the magician's hand, began rapidly and eagerly to gather and tauten his energies. He felt changed, growing; he felt new tensions and new harmonies between himself and the world.

HERMANN HESSE[34]

AIM

This technique is directed to your getting in touch with the overall destiny and purpose of your life as a whole. It goes beyond the one year plan or five year plan you may have for yourself. Rather you will get a feeling for your basic orientation toward the universe and toward God. In a transrational way, you will establish the overall context within which your rational planning takes place.

PREPARE

This visualization exercise will trigger your deepest intuitions about your life's meaning and purpose. You will begin by synchronizing your breathing with your pulse. So find your pulse.

TECHNIQUE

1. Adopt a relaxed yet alert posture. Locate and touch your pulse. Close your eyes, take a deep breath and relax. Breathe in for four beats of your pulse, hold for two beats more, then breathe out for four beats; continue to synchronize your breathing to the 4–2–4 rhythm of your beating pulse.

2. Be still now and open up your heart to receive your true destiny and purpose.

3. Imagine that you are in a rose garden. Experience the colors, the fragrances, the gentle sounds of the garden.

4. Now you are drawn to the middle of the garden where grows a large and beautiful rose bush. See the roots and branches of the bush, and the green leaves gleaming. At the top of the bush is a rosebud which has not opened yet. The bud is still surrounded by its green sepals. Sense the fragrance of the garden and especially of this bush in the center of the garden, crowned by the rosebud at the top which is still closed, but is about to open.

5. Now in very slow motion, see the rosebud begin to open up to the sun. Very slowly the sepals begin to move back. The delicate pink petals, still closed, are revealed to your eyes. The petals are delicate, tender, but you sense the life stirring within them.

6. The petals now begin to stir with that throbbing life.

Slowly the rosebud begins to open out to the sun. You sense the delicate fragrance as the rose starts to blossom.

7. As the petals begin to unfold, be aware of a stirring and blossoming happening at the center of your own self. You feel the depths of your own being stirring and opening out to the light.

8. As you keep visualizing the blossoming of the rose, sense the blossoming of your own being. Know that the rhythm of your own opening out to the light is in tune with the rhythm of the rose's blossoming. It is opening out as you are opening out.

9. The revelation of the beauty of the rose is the revelation of your own beauty.

10. As the rose unfolds and opens to the light and air, so you sense the unfolding of the light and glory of your own true nature and destiny. Breathe the perfume and fragrance of the rose to mingle with the fragrance of your true purpose unfolding in the universe.

11. Now focus your attention on the very center of the rose. There at its center, its life is most intense. Let an image emerge from the center of the rose. This image represents the most beautiful and creative thing that is striving to unfold and blossom in your life right now. This image can be of anything at all. It represents the most meaningful thing coming to light in your life right now. Don't force the image. Don't think about it. Just let it come forth spontaneously.

12. Now stay with the image. Stay with it. Absorb its texture. Let the quality of the image penetrate your being.

13. Be open and receptive to the message that image has for you.

14. Be grateful for this sense of destiny. Be grateful for the direction in which your deepest self is taking you.

15. Take a deep breath. Relax your focus, and when you are ready, come back to ordinary consciousness and open your eyes.

TECHNICAL REFERENCE

The techniques in this book distinguish among three levels of your mind's workings. These levels are presented as useful ways to think about your mind; they are presented as working hypotheses. They are valid only insofar as they are helpful to you. This is not intended as a book about psychological theory. However, the three levels we allude to have a long history in mystical traditions, both east and west.

Most familiar is the level of everyday rational consciousness. This is the ego. This is the level where rational choices are made. You might call it your "guidance system."

Second is the level of subconscious mind. Some call it your organism. The subconscious "tapes" and messages you give yourself have an immense power and control over your behavior. You might call the subconscious your "energy system." Your conscious decisions have little effect when they are at odds with this energy system. That's why people break their New Year's resolutions.

Finally, there is the level of your superconscious mind. This is often named the self or spirit. This dimension of your being transcends your individual ego. Where your conscious mind sees itself as distinct and often at odds with the world around it, your superconscious, your spirit is the part of you that is at one with the world around you, with the universe. It is the part of you where God touches. You might call this level your "universal support system."

The rosebud technique is a method for tapping into this universal support system.

ONE MINUTE MEDITATION

When you lose your focus during the day and feel pulled in many directions, recall the rose and the image emerging from the rose. Let the image of your true nature and purpose pull your life from multiplicity back to unity and focus again. The details of your life make sense to the extent that they are in harmony with the true nature and destiny of your self.

1. Spiritual Techniques
—for Absorbing Sacred Texts

Tool Number 22: Body-Reading (*shindoku*)

Everybody experiences far more than he understands. Yet it is experience, rather than understanding, that influences behavior.

MARSHALL McLUHAN[35]

Enter into the mysteries [of the Scriptures or Holy Books]—to see the scene, to listen to the persons, to smell the fragrance, to taste the sweetness, to touch and embrace and kiss the place where the persons stand or are seated . . . one is approaching the sacred books with one's heart and one's senses.

WILLIAM JOHNSTON[36]

AIM

You will learn a technique for absorbing a sacred text not only into your head, but experientially into your whole body, your whole being. The Buddhist tradition calls this technique, *shindoku,* or "body-reading." It involves the whole self. In the Christian tradition, St. Ignatius of Loyola in his *Spiritual Exercises* called it the method of "Application of the Senses."

PREPARE

This technique invites total involvement of your imagination. You will enact in your mind, as vividly as possible, a story from one of the holy books, in this case from the gospel according to St. Luke, chapter ten. You will not review the story as an outside observer. Rather you are invited to become one of the players in the drama, and to imagine your responses to the place, the event, and especially the people. This is a type of mental role-playing that can reveal to you a lot about yourself.

You don't have to be a biblical fundamentalist to enter effectively into this exercise. Some people will view this story as a literal historical news report issued by a divine wire service. Others might give it the weight of a child's fairy tale, or something in between. You can't fake a faith that you don't have, or deny a faith that you do have. Accept your degree of belief in the sacred book, or the degree of skepticism you have, and enter into the exercise from the faith-standpoint you actually have.

For the true believer, this is a comfortable exercise. The skeptic will best perform the technique as an interesting experiment to see what insight it triggers. At the very least it beats consulting stock market tipsters or the *I Ching* or reading the racing form, exercises to which the most skeptical people can bring the most religious fervor.

TIP

It's the result that counts. Accept *shindoku* as a working hypothesis, test it out for yourself, and see what happens.

TECHNIQUE

1. Begin to involve your body, reading aloud, if possible, the following verses (Lk 10:38–42), recounting the visit of Jesus to his friends, Martha and Mary.

> While they were on their way, Jesus came to a village where a woman named Martha made him welcome in their home.
>
> She had a sister, Mary, who seated herself at the Lord's feet and stayed there listening to his words.

Now Martha was distracted by her many tasks, so she came to him and said,

"Lord, do you not care that my sister has left me to get on with the work by myself? Tell her to come and lend a hand."

But the Lord answered,

"Martha, Martha, you are fretting and fussing about so many things; but one thing is necessary.

"The part that Mary has chosen is best; and it shall not be taken from her."

2. Now close your eyes and prepare for this fantasy technique by using your favorite method of relaxing, composing, and focusing your body and mind.

3. Imagine the home where Martha lives, and the room where the visit takes place. What kind of room is it? See the furnishings. Notice the lighting, the ventilation, the smells. What is the weather outside?

4. Let the scene come to life. See Martha and Mary and Jesus in the room. What are they wearing? What kind of people are they, personality-wise? How do they seem economically—poor, well-to-do, or what? What is the energy level in the room? Does Martha have her act together? Does Mary? Does Jesus?

5. Now put yourself there into the scene. What are you doing? Why are you there? How do you feel as you see the goings-on in the room? How do you feel as you watch Jesus and Martha and Mary relate to each other?

6. See Martha making Jesus welcome in her home. How do you relate to her?

7. See Mary sitting at the feet of Jesus. How do you feel about this?

8. Hear Jesus talking to each of them. How does he seem to feel toward each? How do you feel about the interactions of these people?

9. How do you see yourself taking part in this scene? Whose side are you on? What do you see yourself doing?

10. What do you hear Martha saying to you? What about Mary? Does Jesus say anything to you? Visualize and listen to their responses and yours, and sense the feelings that go through your body.

11. End by spending a quiet moment in that company.

TECHNICAL REFERENCE

Your religious convictions aside, this exercise has value as a psychological technique for triggering a creative insight into a problem, and for seeing yourself in a new perspective.

As an exercise of religious contemplation, it is an excellent method for absorbing a religious teaching into yourself so that it will penetrate your life, your heart, your actions. As Marshall McLuhan pointed out, we experience more than we understand. And it is experience that influences behavior.

Finally, this technique is one way of applying the "hermeneutical method" of biblical interpretation. The Hermeneutical Method of approaching a sacred book is to study the meaning that the text had in its original setting in the context of its original community. But it does not rest there. Taking this original sense of the text as a starting point, the hermeneutical method then invites readers to explore for themselves the meaning that the text has for them in their contemporary life and experience.

ONE MINUTE MEDITATION

Putting yourself in dialogue with a holy book can be a very useful technique when you are stuck in a problem. When your mind is in a rut and you don't know what to do and are going round and round in circles, flip open the Bible at random, or some other holy book. Let the text speak to you from the page. What does it say to your problem? Some people in faith, may experience the Holy Spirit speaking to them through the vehicle of the book. For others, the random text can be a psychological device to provide an unexpected new way of looking at their problem, and the occasion of a fresh new insight.

Tool Number 23: A Christian Koan

> If you would make everything your own, you must want nothing.
>
> SHAKYAMUNI

> The *koan* is intended to be nourished in those recesses of the mind where no logical analysis can ever reach.
>
> D. T. SUZUKI

AIM

How do you deal with problems that just don't make sense? This is another exercise in *shindoku* or "body-reading," a technique for absorbing a text not only into your head but into your body and whole self. The focus of this particular exercise is one of the "kingdom parables" attributed to Jesus. The text expresses an insight that, like a Zen koan, offends and challenges our ordinary rationality and ways of thinking. Since ordinary logic is insufficient for grasping the point of a koan or a parable, all the more is it necessary to use a technique that involves more than intellect alone.

PREPARE

You will use your imagination to become totally absorbed, mind and body, and with all your senses, into the scene, the images, the story recounted in this text. Though the story may offend your sense of logic and justice, let its meaning impact on your total organism. Use your fantasy to immerse yourself totally in the text, and notice your feelings as you respond to this fantasy involvement. You are invited to enter the scene from the very beginning. This is your story.

It is a parable about laborers hired to pick grapes in a vineyard, and how they were paid. Even today, much like in the parable, longshoremen gather in a hiring hall, or migrant workers assemble in a field. The employer or landowner comes and picks out workers who are hired to do the jobs that are lined up for that day. In the parable, workers gather in the town square or marketplace, waiting to be hired out for the day.

TECHNIQUE

1. Begin by reading the following text (Matthew's gospel, 20:1–16):

The kingdom of heaven is like this.

> "There once was a landowner who went out early one morning to hire laborers for his vineyard, and after agreeing to pay them the usual day's wage, he sent them off to work.
>
> "Going out three hours later he saw some more men standing idle in the marketplace.
>
> " 'Go and join the others in the vineyard,' he said, 'and I will pay you a fair wage.' So off they went.
>
> "At midday he went out again. And at three in the afternoon. And made the same arrangement as before.
>
> "An hour before sunset, he went out and found another group standing there, so he said to them:
>
> " 'Why are you standing about like this all day with nothing to do?'
>
> " 'Because no one has hired us,' they replied.

"So he told them, 'Go join the others in the vineyard.'

"When evening fell, the owner of the vineyard said to his steward,

" 'Call the laborers and give them their pay, beginning with those who came last and ending with the first.'

"Those who started to work an hour before sunset came forward, and were paid the full day's wage.

"When it was the turn of the men who had come first, they expected something extra, but were paid the same amount as the others.

"As they took it, they grumbled at their employer,

" 'These latecomers have done only one hour's work. You have put them on a level with us who have sweated the whole day long in the blazing sun!'

"The owner turned to one of them and said,

" 'My friend, I am not being unfair to you. You agreed on the usual wage for the day, did you not? Take your pay and go home. I choose to pay the last man the same as you. Surely I am free to do what I like with my own money. Why be jealous, because I am kind?'

"Thus will the last be first, and the first last."

2. Close your eyes and ready your mind and body to enter into the fantasy.

3. Transport yourself in your imagination to a small country village. This is grape country. All around this area are vineyards owned by local wine-growers. You get up early this morning and put on your work clothes. You hope to be hired out to work in one of the vineyards today. You need the money. See yourself walking in the early morning air to the town square where you join the others waiting to be hired.

4. As you walk, note the weather, the sounds, the smells, the

colors. What is the mood of the people with you? How do you feel?

5. The winegrower comes to pick out laborers. You are one of the first to be hired. Note how you feel when he points to you and agrees to take you on for the usual day's wage.

6. Imagine your walk to the vineyard with the other workers, your receiving your work assignment. How does it feel as you work: the digging, the weeding, the pruning? How do you interact with the dirt, the vines, the heat, the insects, the stooping the bending, the crawling, the reaching? How are you relating to your fellow workers, and with your boss?

7. You've been working three hours. Feel your aches, pains, thirst, hunger. At the three hour mark, a new crew comes to join you. How do you feel about these newcomers?

8. It's now three in the afternoon. You've been there all morning and into the afternoon. How have you survived the heat of the day? You notice at three o'clock yet another new crew coming in. You see them start to work. How do you feel about these newcomers? You work on.

9. The sun is low in the sky. It's an hour before sunset and quitting time. How does your body feel now? What are you thinking? With only an hour to go, you see a new crew coming in and starting to work. What are your feelings about this new group?

10. Finally sunset; twilight falls; a cool breeze sets in. You hear a bell ending the workday. You all gather around a platform in the middle of the field to get your pay.

11. Those who began to work an hour ago are called forward. A full day's pay is announced for them. And they step up to receive it. How do you feel?

12. Next those who came at three. Full pay for them is announced and they step up to receive it. How do you feel?

13. Next those who came late in the morning receive a full day's pay. How do you feel now? Finally you and your group come forward to receive your agreed upon wage, a full day's pay for your full day's work. Hear the angry reactions of your fellow workers.

14. Hear the words of your employer, "My friend, I am not being unfair to you. You agreed on the usual wage for the day, did you not? Take your pay and go home. I choose to pay the last man the same as you. Surely I am free to do what I like with my own money. Why be jealous because I am kind?" How do these words make you feel?

15. Reflect on the words of Jesus about the kingdom of heaven: "Thus will the last be first and the first last."

TECHNICAL REFERENCE

The parables of Jesus can be viewed as the Christian version of the Zen koan. Their insights are paradoxical. They are an affront to ordinary rationality. You bypass rational thought by immersing yourself in the parable through the body-reading or "application of the senses." Not trapped in the dead end of your ordinary logic, you are opened up to the possibility of receiving unexpected insight from new perspectives you wouldn't ordinarily dream of. Since Jesus' teaching about the kingdom, the rule of the Father, is so often a reversal of human logic, techniques for dealing with and absorbing paradoxical insight are essential for grasping his meaning.

ONE MINUTE MEDITATION

An affront to the normal mindset can be a challenge to broaden your perspective and enhance your survivability. On the purely psychological level, paradox can be a path to insight. Turn the negatives in your life on their head: decide to view them as positives. Note that the labels come from you anyway. The realities are simply there—unlabeled. Ask, "What is there for me to learn here?" "What good purpose can be served by this?" "How can I maximize the potential of this happening?"

Nasrudin's wife burst into the Mulla's room and cried, "Mulla, your donkey has disappeared!" The Mulla calmly looked up and replied, "Thank goodness I wasn't on it at the time, otherwise I would have disappeared too."

2. Psychological Techniques

Tool Number 24: Fantasy Vacation

When the heart weeps for what it has lost
The spirit laughs for what it has found.

SUFI SAYING[37]

Daydreams are dangerous only when the dreamer cannot distinguish between sense reality and fantasy reality, or when he has no power to turn his dreams off and on at will.

ANTHONY DE MELLO[38]

AIM

You will learn that your power of fantasy is alive and well. You will exercise it in a most pleasant way. You will see how fantasy can be directly turned to the service of spiritual growth.

This is a Monday morning kind of exercise. You will learn to leave a holiday behind, without leaving behind, too, the refreshment, strength and vigor the holiday was meant to give you.

PREPARE

This technique invites you to dream about good times you have had. You are invited to imagine a place, a time, and people, where you were really really yourself, happy, supported, peaceful, and strong. You will time travel to a place in your past where you experienced great happiness and inner security and strength.

TRAP

Make this not a thought trip, but a fantasy trip. Actually relive that place, that experience, that place in all its detail. Recreate the feelings, the sensations, the relationships, and the insights that make that place and time stand out in your life.

TECHNIQUE

1. Settle yourself into a relaxed alert posture. Block your eyes and ears with your fingers and thumbs, and take ten deep breaths. Then sit, eyes closed, hands on your lap, and attend to the sensations in your body, beginning at the top of your head.

2. Without using labels, be aware and feel the exact sensation in each part and place in your body. If there is tension, attend closely to it, exactly how it feels. If a part feels numb, see if you can notice *some* sensation there. If you note a pain or an ache, experience it in precise detail; notice all the different kinds of sensations that go to make up this one aching sensation. Keep moving your attention down through your body, down to the tips of your toes in your stockings.

3. Begin now to tap your imagination and power of fantasy. Withdraw to a time and a place and a happening where you experienced great joy and happiness. Relive that event in all its detail. Don't "think" about it, but *be* there again. Recreate the colors and the sounds; hear the voices.

4. Experience once again the sensations and feelings in your body that you felt at that time and place.

5. Relive the joy. Recreate your responses to the people and the surroundings. Recreate once again their responses to you.

6. Relax and enjoy your fantasy of this happy time and place. Smell the fragrances, taste the flavors, feel the touches, recreate the joy. Stay with this fantasy experience for a few moments.

7. Now switch your focus. Still relaxed, with eyes closed, return your attention to this room, this day, this time, right now. Notice all the details of your situation right here. What do you hear? Note again the sensations throughout your body. How have they changed?

8. Especially, note your feelings now at this time and place. Pay attention to exactly what feelings you are experiencing right now. Stay with this for a few minutes.

9. Switch back again in fantasy to that other happy place and time. Recreate that experience again in all its sensuous detail. Pay particular attention to your feelings in that place. Have your feelings changed? Has that place changed at all? Enjoy this fantasy again.

10. Then switch back to this room and this time. What do you feel now? Notice any changes.

11. Switch back and forth from the fantasy place and time to this present place and time. Each time, note your feelings. Be aware of how your feelings change. Keep moving from then and there to here and now, until you are ready to end this exercise.

TECHNICAL REFERENCE

Your fantasy life has an unbelievably powerful effect on your feelings, actions and life. Your mental imagery shapes your emotions and your decisions. It is a psychological truism that feelings should not be denied. But feelings can be controlled, indirectly, by controlling the images that you entertain in your mind. You have the power to choose which images will energize your feelings, choices, and actions.

The bottom line is that you need not be the victim of your feelings. Your mind can deal with only one thought or image at a time. When a depressing thought drags your feelings down, change the thought, change the image. An upbeat image yields upbeat feelings. You can choose your feelings by choosing your thoughts. You are in control.

Undeniably, feelings sometimes overwhelm such techniques for controlling them indirectly. Even so, you still need not be the victim of your feelings. Unlike feelings, your behavior is under your direct control. It can help to view feelings as internal weather. Wait long enough, and the emotional weather will change. Meanwhile, you get on with your life. Even though the weather outside isn't ideal, you go to work and you go to play each day. No need either to wait for ideal emotional weather inside, before you go to work or go to play. Just do what you have to do, and let the low pressure and high pressure currents of your emotional weather sort themselves out, just as you let the lows and highs of outdoor weather sort themselves out as you go about with your life.

TIP

How can I stop myself from boozing?
Don't put alcohol in your mouth.
—DYER

ONE MINUTE MEDITATION

Recall a time a place where you felt very close to God or very attuned to the universe, a favorite retreat of your very own where you felt great peace and harmony—a seashore perhaps, a starlit night, a secret hiding place. Treat yourself from time to time with a short spiritual vacation. Using all your senses, recapture and relive in your fantasy every detail of your spiritual experience in that special place.

Tool Number 25: Your Power of Choice

Freedom is the right to create for yourself the alternatives of choice. Without the possibility of choice and the exercise of choice, a man is not a man, but a member, an instrument, a thing.

ARCHIBALD MACLEISH[39]

Men have never fully used the powers they possess to advance the good in life, because they have waited upon some power external to themselves and to nature to do the work they are responsible for doing.

JOHN DEWEY

AIM

You will learn one way to make effective decisions without imposing on yourself your customary self-limiting assumptions.

PREPARE

You will make three lists, ten items in each list. This technique works with your self-conscious mind, the part of you that analyzes, defines, reasons, decides, and chooses. The choices you make concern your own life. You are the expert here.

First list ten things that work well in your life and that you like about your life. Then list ten things that are not working in your life, and that you do not like. On your third list, take each item that is not working and that you don't like, and write down instead its opposite, i.e. write down the result that you *would* like to see working in your life instead. After you write down

128

each positive result, cross out the corresponding negative item from the second list. Label the third list "My Creative Choices and Commitments" or "Choices I Make About the Results I Want To Create in My Life."

TRAPS

First, let's critique the list to make sure that your choices are framed so that they will be effective.

(1) It is a trap to choose what you do *not* want. The choices should be positive. Choose what you *do* want, not what you *don't* want. Choose to "be a slim person" rather than to "give up sweets." Choose "healthy lungs and sensitive taste buds" rather than "no more cigarettes." Choose a "fulfilling intimate relationship" rather than "dump my spouse."

(2) Eliminate items from your list that refer to actions and choices that have to be made by other people. This is not about manipulating others. It's about your own choices. Don't choose that your father should quit abusing alcohol; do choose the response you would like to create for yourself vis-à-vis your father. Don't choose that X should fall in love with you; do choose the kind of loving relationship you'd like to bring about in your life.

(3) It is a trap to choose things that refer to the *process* of achieving your goals. Choose, rather, the goals and results themselves. Choose the *what* of the results, not the *how to*. If you choose process, it's the process you will get, not the results you really want. If you want a particular job, choose the job; don't choose to "have good interviews." I have known people who have gotten lost in the process of going from good interview to good interview and lost sight of the end result, the job itself. There are many ways of getting a job besides good interviews. Your uncle can put in a good word for you. The current job-holder can drop dead just before you walk in the door. You can

be the minority candidate that saves the company from a law-suit. Or, of course, you can have a good interview.

(4) It is a trap to unnecessarily limit yourself. What you want is one thing. What you think is possible is another. If you want it, go for it, without prematurely closing down possibilities.

TIPS

(1) Make the result you choose as specific as possible. If you want a car, choose model, make and color. And give the chosen result a time frame: by exactly what date do you want exactly what to happen?

(2) Decide whether you really want this result. Test question: if you could have it now, would you take it? Do you have any doubts?

TECHNIQUE

Once you have critiqued and framed your choices so that they are truly the positive, specific, results you want, then take each item in turn and choose it. Go for it without reservations. Say to yourself out loud: "I choose X. I totally direct and commit my life to achieving this goal." You know when you have made a real choice, a real commitment. There's a little "click" in your consciousness. A light goes on. You know your life will not be the same again, because you've embarked on a new path.

Read the list of choices every night before you go to bed, ratifying your choices and firm commitment to them.

TECHNICAL REFERENCE

There are two kinds of decision-making: (1) decisions by de-fault, and (2) decisions by choice. Decisions by default inher-ently give rise to conflict, and must fail. Decisions by choice

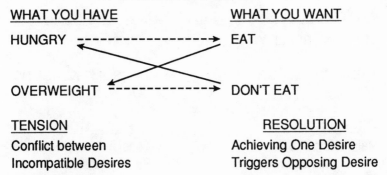

Diagram One: Decisions by Default
SYSTEMIC CONFLICT

WHAT YOU HAVE	WHAT YOU WANT
HUNGRY	EAT
OVERWEIGHT	DON'T EAT

TENSION	RESOLUTION
Conflict between	Achieving One Desire
Incompatible Desires	Triggers Opposing Desire

inevitably will create the results you want. Let's outline the structure of each decision-making procedure.[40]

See Diagram One. Decisions by Default can't work. You are jerked back and forth by achieving incompatible desires. You are hungry, you want to eat. But eating makes you overweight. You don't want this, so you don't eat. Not eating resolves overweight, but it makes you hungry. So once again you eat. Decision by default makes you a ping-pong ball to irreconcilable desires. The resolution of one desire creates need in the opposite desire, creating conflict without end.

See Diagram Two. Decision by Choice must work. You choose the result that you want to create. You choose "a slim energetic you"—that is your vision. But at the same time, you keep a clear-eyed focus on what your current reality is, "the overweight sluggish you"—that is what you now have. Note that you choose the result, not the process. You don't choose to give up ice cream or to starve yourself. No, you choose the kind of body you want to have. But you don't deny your present reality either. The dissonance between your present reality and your vision creates tension.

Diagram Two: Decisions by Choice
CREATIVE DISSONANCE

WHAT YOU HAVE	RESULT YOU CHOOSE TO CREATE
CURRENT REALITY ----------▸	VISION
THE HEAVY SLUGGISH --------▸ YOU	THE SLIM ENERGETIC YOU
TENSION Maintaining Creative Dissonance Between Current Reality and Vision	RESOLUTION Tension Resolved in Favor of Vision Achieved

It is important to maintain this tension. The effort to resolve the tension is what sparks the creative energy that will bring about your vision. As you keep a clear eye on the vision, it will become increasingly uncomfortable to act in ways that are incompatible with the vision. It doesn't feel right for this slim energetic you so clearly in your chosen self-image to be lying around evening after evening eating potato chips and ice cream while watching TV. And your behavior slowly, often in surprising ways, begins to conform to the vision. It becomes more comfortable to conform to the vision than it is to experience the tension between your vision and current reality. So the tension gets resolved as you with increasing momentum bring the vision to fruition.

So in decision by choice, you choose to change your current reality, and thereby set up a creative dissonance between where you are and where you want to be. There are only two ways to resolve this tension. One is by bringing your vision to fruition: you succeed in becoming the slim energetic self you want to be. The vision becomes your current reality. Or you can give up your vision and rest in your current reality, your overweight sluggish self. As long as you maintain your commitment to your choice, you keep the creative tension alive, and you cannot but succeed.

ONE MINUTE MEDITATION

When in the course of your daily living, things are not going well for you, and you are not getting the results that you want, this is the time to pause and reaffirm your choice, as follows:

(1) Pause and clearly note what is actually going on that is out of sync with what you want. You are getting clear about current reality.

(2) Choose clearly the results that you want, the vision.

(3) Now that you have reestablished the creative tension, just go on to something else.

No guilt trips, no regrets, no beating yourself for having failed. You have reaffirmed your direction. So be at peace, trust yourself and go on living.

If you love someone or want something, and things are not responding as you would like, recall this Sufi saying:

If you love something, let it go. If it returns to you it is yours. If it doesn't, it never was yours to begin with.

Tool Number 26: Commitment Without Will Power

The real function of will is to direct, not to impose.

PIERO FERRUCCI[41]

Unawareness of one's feet is a mark of shoes that fit. Unawareness of one's waist is the mark of a belt that fits. Unawareness of right and wrong is the mark of a mind at ease.

CHUANG TZU[42]

AIM

This is a technique about choice. The aim is to pick a goal you truly want, and set all your energy and commitment in motion toward achieving that goal. We assume that your will, your power of choice is your guidance system. It is not your energy system. Your choice sets your direction, your goal. This is not will *power*. You don't draw on your will for the power to achieve your goal. To choose your goal is one thing. The process of how you will achieve it is something else. Choose the "what," not the "how."

PREPARE

Here is an example of the difference between choice and will power. A woman decided she would use willpower to force herself to stop smoking. With tremendous will power, she

134

stopped by brute force. Her withdrawal was an agony. For six years she had nightmares about smoking. She was a smoker without a cigarette. One day at a party she was persuaded to light up. She started right back at two packs a day, and could not force herself to stop again. Then one day she decided, "No more will power." She decided to become a non-smoker, but without forcing herself. She began to quietly study her smoking behavior.

I just started noting when I wanted to smoke and what it felt like when I lit up. I decided that any time I wanted a cigarette I would have one, but I also decided to become very, very aware of when the desire stopped, and to put out the cigarette as soon as I didn't want it any more. I became hyperaware of just what was going on within me. It was not just body, and it was not just mind; it was a gestalt of body and mind. They were of one piece when I wanted a cigarette, and when I took my first puff.

I became fascinated with this process and thought about it a lot. I thought, "Smoking is not natural. It is acquired, so it can be disacquired."

I didn't concern myself with the dynamics of what motivated me to start when I was a kid, or what the Freudian meaning of the recurring nightmares were. I am sure that there was a lot of sexual and other symbolism in the dreams, but I just concentrated on what was happening when I smoked.

Then to my surprise, on the third morning, when I started to smoke my favorite cigarette of the day with my breakfast coffee, it tasted bad. I put it out and started another, but it tasted bad too. I got another pack, thinking that maybe there was something wrong with the cigarettes, but they were bad too. I only wanted a cigarette twice more that day, once the next day, and after that I just didn't want to smoke. I carried a pack around for months in case I should want one but I never have. It's been years now, and even in moments of stress it never occurs to me to smoke.[43]

No longer was she a smoker deprived by her will power. She had become her goal, namely, a non-smoker who simply did not relate to cigarettes. Her decision to quit provided her with a direction. But the energy to stop came not from will power but from *vipassana,* the power of awareness and attention.

Before you start on this technique, choose a goal that you would like to work on. Let it be something that is important to you, something that is not an empty possibility, a mere hope, or a "should."

In this exercise, you will visualize your path toward that goal. You will calmly and clearly commit yourself to it, set your self in your chosen direction.

TECHNIQUE

1. Before you embark on this exercise of conscious choice and commitment, energize and focus yourself as follows. Stand, relaxed, feet solidly planted, eyes open. You have a sense of being very much present here and now.

2. Feel the solid floor beneath you; focus on the solid floor; "see" it with your feet. Then feel the solidness beneath you for miles and miles.

3. Shift your attention to the top of your head; sense with your head the space between you and the ceiling; sense the space above the ceiling, the space above the ceiling to the infinite edge of the universe.

4. Return your attention to the room, and notice the space around you, the forms, the colors, the people.

5. Pay attention now to the sounds around you, the sounds outside.

6. Now attend to the sounds inside you; sense the beating of your heart.

7. Fully present to yourself and the world, audibly exhale as you sit down.

8. Close your eyes. Focus now on the goal you are committing yourself to today. Let an image, vague or definite, spontaneously emerge that symbolizes this goal for you. It can be anything at all—a person, a natural object, an animal, anything.[44]

9. Now see yourself standing at the foot of a hill. In front of you is a long straight clear path leading to the top of the hill. On the hilltop in the distance you see the image that symbolizes your goal.

10. Begin to proceed on your path to the goal. On both sides of the path you see and hear and feel various entities that will try to lure you off the path and prevent your reaching the top.

11. They will try to do anything. There is one thing they cannot do. They cannot block your path. Your path remains straight and clear before you.

12. You continue up the path toward your goal. Along the sides, you perceive situations in your life, persons, feelings, distracting goals. These try to turn you aside, to discourage you, to frighten you, to seduce you. One thing they cannot do. They cannot block your path. It remains straight and clear before you.

13. Continue to proceed up the path toward your goal. Feel the pull of the situations, and feelings, and beings that try to divert you. You can even dialogue with them, notice their strategy. But you move on. You are clear effortless will. You are committed to your direction and goal. Aware of the forces along the sides, continue to move easily up the path. You are clear effortless will.

14. When you reach the top, stay with your image of purpose achieved. Experience yourself possessing your goal. Savor its meaning. Open yourself up to everything it has to say to you.

15. Be grateful for your clear calm commitment. Know that your clear choice without effort will direct your energies toward all your goals.

TECHNICAL REFERENCE

This technique shows the interplay of conscious, superconscious and subconscious dimensions in bringing your goals to fruition. The rationally chosen conscious goal was aligned with your deep self's true destiny, represented by the spontaneously emerging image of your goal. This keeps you from being at odds with yourself, as when you choose a goal that just "isn't you," usually under pressure to please someone else or to please your own perfectionism. When the goal is subsumed under your true nature and purpose, you tap into a vast reservoir of power propelling you toward your destiny. And, finally, the visualization of your journey up the hill brings your subconscious energies to bear on your success.

Note that focusing on one goal, as you did in this technique, has an overflow effectively channeling your energy and commitment toward achieving all your consciously chosen goals. So it is very useful to work intensively toward the achieving of a single goal, though, of course, the technique can also be used for other targets.

ONE MINUTE MEDITATION

From time to time throughout the day, recall the image of your goal, and direct your will and commitment to it. This is an especially useful exercise before going to sleep at night, or upon awakening in the morning.

Tool Number 27: Self-Creation

At twenty you have the face you were born with; at forty you have the face you have created for yourself.

OLD SAYING

No one can make you feel inferior without your consent.

ELEANOR ROOSEVELT

AIM

You will learn how to direct your subconscious to guide you positively and energize you creatively in your everyday conscious decisions. You will focus on your self-image, and on the creation of a positive self-image.

PREPARE

Your subconscious is 100% agreeable and obedient to the suggestions that you give it (more on this later). As with the other techniques, don't take this on faith. Accept it as a working hypothesis, and test it out for yourself.

It will be important to become as relaxed and open as possible so as to have your subconscious mind receptive to your suggestions. You will be giving your subconscious a clear signal to guide your life with a positive self-image, without contradiction or ambiguity.

This is a visualization technique. Note two things about this visualization. (1) You are going to visualize the person you want to be: your looks, your health, your social life, your accomplishments, your power, your harmony, your freedom. It is important to see this image as already present, as something you have now, not something that lies in the future. See your ideal self-image as something you already possess right now. (2) It is important to bring your feelings to bear in the creation of your ideal self-image. Emotions are a powerful reinforcer of the suggestions you give to the subconscious. So let yourself feel just terrific about the positive self-image you create.

TRAP

It is a mistake to *try hard* to convince your subconscious about anything. Your subconscious is a pushover. Just tell it, and it will agree. If you *try hard* to convince your subconscious, your subconscious will take this as a suggestion: "Yes, you really have to try hard to convince me." So just very simply tell your subconscious what to believe; know that it is a pushover.

TECHNIQUE

1. Divide this exercise into two equal parts. First, use your preferred method for entering into a state of deep relaxation. For example, slowly move your attention throughout your whole body, noting the feelings and sensations in each part. Or take five minutes to play the breathing game, counting every single breath from one to ten as you exhale.

2. Now make an affirmation, a suggestion to your subconscious. In a relaxed and non-pressing way, repeat the following in your mind: "I have the ability and power to live a positive creative life. I have that power right now. This ability penetrates all aspects of my life experience." I am full . . . whole . . . and in perfect balance. Furthermore, "I am worthy of good and great success in all my undertakings."

3. Next you will begin to teach your self-conscious mind your ideal self-image. Begin to experience how you feel when you are this ideal person. Concentrate on what a great sense of freedom and power you have when you are being this perfect self-image.

4. It is *essential* that you experience this self-image as *present now,* as *already achieved,* not as something that lies in the future. Otherwise the subconscious will get the message that the ideal you is to remain a future ideal, never to be achieved. So notice how good you feel *now* . . . how happy . . . how contented . . . how creative. Put a smile on your face. When you smile, your subconscious says "yes" to your happiness. Put a big smile on your face.

5. Now choose any aspect of this positive that you want, and concentrate on that.

6. Next you will teach your subconscious a key suggestion that will make it able to call forth this ideal self-image immediately and automatically whenever you want. Again, you will address the subconscious directly. In a relaxed and non-pressured way, say the following in your mind: "Subconscious, when I say to you my name [*now say your own name*], this perfect self-image will automatically and immediately become manifest on all levels of my being."

7. Reinforce this suggestion by repeating it once again.

8. Now say your name, and immediately become that self-image. Feel and experience it fully for a few seconds.

9. Quietly come back to ordinary consciousness, and open your eyes.

TECHNICAL REFERENCE

You are invited to accept as a working hypothesis this power of your subconscious. This is not the place to make metaphysical or psychological claims about the existence of a mental power or faculty distinct from the conscious mind. All we do is make what appears to be a useful postulate, and invite you to test it for yourself. We make the assumption that there is an aspect of the mind's functioning that is susceptible to suggestion and able to influence powerfully your conscious decisions and actions. We call this aspect or mechanism of mind the subconscious. It has the following characteristics which you can test for yourself.

First, it maintains a clear record of every detail of your life, and of every thought you have ever had. Indeed many things that you don't recall consciously perceiving are recorded in great detail subconsciously.

Second, it has no thoughts of its own, but it deduces conclusions from what is fed to it from your experiences, actions, and suggestions. It operates deductively. It is the responsive part of the mind.   ·

Third, the conclusions it draws tend to appear in our life experience. That's why suggestions given to the subconscious, for better or for worse, are so powerful.

Fourth, it is essentially dumb and uncritical. It says "yes" to all the input it receives, and immediately strives to create or manifest what it concludes from the input.

Finally, since the subconscious is completely uncritical, it is necessary to give it clear and unambiguous suggestions if you want to draw effectively on its power. If you give it contradictory suggestions, the subconscious will accept the contradiction uncritically, and operate at cross-purposes with itself. In a word, suggestions given to the subconscious are self-fulfilling prophecies.

For example, you say, "I want a job in sales at Ajax Computer Corporation," and your subconscious says "yes" and begins to energize you toward that goal. But you also say, "I am a woman, and Ajax Computer Corporation would never hire a woman in sales," and your subconscious says "yes" and proceeds to ensure that being a woman blocks you from the job.

Compare this suggestion: "I want a job in sales at Ajax Computer Corporation, and being a woman makes me a unique and valuable candidate for the position." The subconscious says "yes" and proceeds to make your femaleness an asset as it propels you toward the job.

ONE MINUTE MEDITATION

During the day or night, when you feel particularly unfocused, anxious, or powerless, you have at your command a tool to pull yourself together and bring your energies back into focus. Take a deep breath and say your own name. Your subconscious will immediately and automatically manifest in you the wholeness, the balance, the energy of your positive self-image.

Tool Number 28: The "Now" of Your Life

To live in the present is like proposing to sit on a pin. It is too minute, it is too slight a support, it is too uncomfortable a posture, and it is of necessity followed immediately by totally different experiences, analogous to those of jumping up with a yell.

CHESTERTON[45]

To pay attention, but not to concentrate, to be still, and at the same time to let go. To stop rehearsing, stop the fantasies. Look with your eyes. I don't know what there is to see. Listen with your ears. Everything is alive. Perhaps you can hear it being alive. Sit there . . . by missing the minute, you are missing everything, because all you have is that minute.

JOAN BAEZ[46]

AIM

You will master a technique for bringing your creative power to bear on the present moment. The now is where you live. It is the only place you can self-consciously create the results you have chosen to bring about in your life.

PREPARE

Forgive yourself for the negatives in your past. Without repressing your regrets, don't dwell on them either. When you live in the past, you give it power. The past becomes a self-fulfilling prophecy to be recreated in your future.

You will be instructing your subconscious to respond to your

144

present choices. Recall the "weakness" of your subconscious, how susceptible it is to your suggestions. Recall the strength of your subconscious, the immense energy it devotes to manifesting and translating your suggestions into your life. So address the subconscious calmly and clearly. Give it the suggestions that you choose to make into self-fulfilling prophecies.

TIP

In a guided technique like the following, it can be helpful to tape the instructions or have someone read them to you. This is not essential; you can also cue yourself.

TECHNIQUE

1. Close your eyes, take a deep breath and relax. Imagine that you are standing before an elevator. You enter, the doors close, and you notice that you are on the 100th floor. The elevator begins to move down. As you descend floor by floor to the basement, you become more and more relaxed. When you come to the basement, you will be in a very deep state of relaxation, and you will have excellent and easy communication between your conscious mind and your subconscious mind.

2. You are moving down to floor 99, 98, 97, 96, 95, 94, 93, 92, 91, 90, and down to 80 . . . , 70, 60, 50, 40, 30, 20, 10, down to 9, and you are now very relaxed. Deeper you go to 8, 7, 6, 5, 4, 3, 2, 1, to the basement which is zero, and you are in a very deep state of relaxation. Take a deep breath, and as you exhale, allow yourself to go even deeper. You are now in a very pleasant state of deep relaxation. Without effort, your subconscious is in deep rapport with your conscious mind.

3. Now repeat in your mind the following suggestion to your subconscious: "Subconscious, you are directed to focus and

respond to my present choices. The most powerful moment of my life is right now."

4. Repeat this suggestion to your subconscious twice again.

5. Next, instruct your subconscious as follows: "Subconscious, when I say to you the words 'right now,' you will respond to my conscious choices."

6. Repeat to your subconscious the words "right now" and experience your subconscious focusing on the most powerful moment of your life which is right now.

7. Take a deep breath and at your own pace come back to ordinary consciousness and open your eyes.

TECHNICAL REFERENCE

Recall that the direction of your life is supplied by the conscious choices you make. But the energy comes from the subconscious tapes that the mind rehearses in the background. So it is essential that the conscious and subconscious be attuned to each other. This technique is a short-cut way of accomplishing this attunement.

ONE MINUTE MEDITATION

When daydreams about the past or worries about the future are pulling you away from the task at hand, repeat to yourself the words "right now" to focus the energy of your creative choices on your present action. Now is the only moment that counts. Now is when your life happens. If each moment is a success, your whole life is a success.

III. Interpreting Religious Experience

To shop in today's psychospiritual "supermarket" is to encounter a confounding diversity of offerings. For the individual with a genuine hunger for truth, reality, spirit, soul, self, God, oneness, freedom, being, and meaning, the task of choosing among these offerings is intricate and subtle, and not without an element of peril.[47]

People say that what we're all seeking is a meaning for life. I don't think that's what we're really seeking. I think that what we're seeking is an experience of being alive, so that our life experiences on the purely physical plane will have resonances within our own innermost being and reality, that we actually feel the rapture of being alive.

JOSEPH CAMPBELL[48]

A. Problems of Interpretation

Most of the techniques in this book are part and parcel of long-standing mystical traditions. People can engage in these practices using the same postures and positions, and following the same rules and procedures. And such people will often use similar terms to describe exactly what they experienced during the meditation period. One might conclude that they are all doing pretty much the same thing.

But this facade of unity quickly breaks down when people are asked to interpret what the experience meant to them in theological, metaphysical, or even psychological terms. We tend to think that there are a half dozen or perhaps a dozen great world religions. A Jesuit psychotherapist once told me that he had reached the conclusion that there are as many religions as there are people. And the same could doubtlessly be said about philosophies of life, metaphysical theories and cosmologies.

The truth of the matter is that people interpret the same events and experiences in startlingly different ways. This is true even of contemporary everyday experiences, and much more true of private "religious" experiences. Perhaps the reason we can maintain the illusion of sharing a similar experiential world is that we seldom really listen to what someone else is saying about that world. We bracket out the differences and discrepancies. Be that as it may, I tried, admittedly with limited success, to present the techniques in this book with as little theological and metaphysical baggage as possible. The aim was to introduce you to these spiritual transformational techniques, but to present them as working hypotheses—orthopraxy over orthodoxy, if you will. Their utility for you was yours alone to judge. And interpretation of their meanings, theological or otherwise, was yours alone to make.

The hands-off policy regarding interpretation of mystical experience has its problems. The emergence of trash TV attests to the fact that there is no interpretation or perspective on experience so bizarre that there isn't someone out there who will cheerfully defend it. Much as I respect your right to interpret your experience as you like, I will be a wee bit skeptical if you emerge from mantra meditation with the claim that a chieftain's wife named Suia has just channelled you a message from the Early Bronze Age about next month's municipal election.

On the other hand it is not easy to legislate how people are to interpret experience, though this is not from lack of trying. Ayatollahs and fundamentalists of all stripes, secular humanists and doctrinaire atheists strive to impose correct theologies and anti-theologies. Anti-defamation leagues on all sides and "consciousness-raising" groups for every special interest strive to enforce their versions of politically correct thinking, and even of politically correct language. There is no shortage of thought police. But it is a futile game. Ironically enough, the thought police often end up as the most entertaining players on the very trash TV it is their mission in life to control.

So, by way of trying to steer a middle course between trash TV and thought police, I offer some categories for interpretation of mystical experience that I have found useful. It is done in the spirit of getting the cards out on the table. I'll do it by way of question and answer.

B. Meditation vs. Day-Dreaming

What's the difference between so-called "awareness" meditation and doing nothing at all? Isn't meditation as much a waste of time as idle day-dreaming is?

The short answer is to meditate and see for yourself. The longer answer lies in the following four principles. I'll focus on *vipassana* meditation which uses thought or breathing or sounds as its object. Such meditation seems the antithesis of anything practical. These principles give the rationale for the claim that *vipassana* is one of the best practical uses to which you can put your time.

Principle 1. *Clear awareness is preferable to clouded or fuzzy awareness.* The Principle of Clarity urges you to be as alert and precise as possible about your thoughts and feelings. There is a certain clarity when you say, "I'm feeling listless." You are more clear when you say, "There is a dull ache in my head, my eyes are trying to close, and there is a heaviness in my stomach." There is even more clarity when you recall the sequences of thoughts and accompanying feelings that brought on the onset of the listless sensations. Mindfulness means that there is lucid, detailed, articulate transparency to your consciousness of what is happening in you. And there is a value judgment that knowing the truth about one's internal stream of consciousness is preferable to being inured to it.

Principle 2. *Allowing the flow of mind-body processes to proceed unhindered is preferable to blocking or freezing them.* The Principle of Neutrality urges you to become a matter-of-fact neutral observer of yourself. This is akin to the Taoist doctrine of *wu wei* (letting be). Meditation points not merely to awareness, but to accepting what you become aware of. It is the opposite of our all too common tendency to deny, to block, to grasp. In the Buddhist view, such resisting is the source of limitation and all suffering. "Pain" is a sensation; "suffering" lies in resistance to pain. The second principle urges the moment by moment acceptance of what is revealed to the heightened clarity that comes with meditation.

Principle 3. *If you follow the first two principles, you will notice important transformations taking place in you spontaneously.* The Principle of Transformation teaches that precise observation without hindrance and distortion brings realization and positive transformation. There is a transformative power in the very fact of awareness and your non-resistance to it. You don't have to *try* to change. The very mindfulness itself effects the change. Meditation, freeing you from the trap of your mind-body processes, transforms moment to moment awareness and acceptance to moment to moment fulfillment.

Principle 4. *When you react to the meditation process, be it with annoyance, restlessness, boredom, or bliss, make these reactions themselves also the object of your even-handed awareness.* The Principle of Self-Correction urges you to apply the same two principles to the process of meditation itself. *Vipassana* is a self-corrective process. Responses and problems that you have with awareness will be resolved by awareness of these responses and problems. Just consistently apply the first two principles, and transformation will take care of itself, and meditation will take care of itself as well, when even your responses to *it* become the object of your awareness.

Furthermore, consideration of individual transformation should be elevated to the cosmic level. We walk the earth with other human beings, with all other living creatures, and indeed the earth itself is part of us. The welfare of the whole ecosphere is bound up with the sensibilities and realization of its human component. Humans have a special power to shape, direct, create (or destroy) the whole. In a sense the role of the human race is to be the sensitive nerve ends of nature. The inner development of human beings is an essential prerequisite for fulfilling this cosmic duty. It is a cliché that our scientific, technological, and military advances have outstripped our ability to control them. Only spiritual development which reveals the secrets of self-realization brings the wisdom for realization of the ecological whole. If humans are not up to the task, the penalty may be their extinction in favor of another species that will better fulfill this role. Such are nature's inexorable laws.

C. Psychology vs. Spirituality

What is the difference between psychological growth and spiritual growth? Don't they come down to pretty much the same thing?

It is difficult to compartmentalize psychology, which etymologically means the "science of the soul" after all, as something apart from spirituality. Many people do assimilate spiritual growth to psychological health and maturity. Norman Vincent Peale and Robert Schuller are examples of such psychologizers of religious experience. Spiritual growth gets assimilated to the power of positive thinking and psychological wellness. The transcendental meditation movement and Werner Erhard's EST training [now called "The Forum"] are also psychologizers of mystical experience that remain firmly at the naturalistic level. While these latter do not present a religious facade, they use categories of transformation and enlightenment understood in psychological terms. It is hard to envisage psychological health as the enemy to holiness. Still, it is important to distinguish the two, lest what is unique to the spiritual dimension and spiritual growth get reduced out by being psychologized.

Psychology is about historical animal humanity, our human incarnation, as it were. Psychological therapies are designed to help dysfunctional people function effectively within the context of their incarnate lives. Therapy gets people to stand on their own two feet able to take responsibility for their lives. Therapy solves problems and resolves conflicts. Ideally, a psychological problem is not something you want to devote your life to resolving.

Spirituality is about transcending our animal humanity, going beyond our history-bound incarnate existence. Psychotherapy is a means to an end. The spiritual quest for transcendence is an end in itself. Psychological problems present themselves to be solved, fixed. Spiritual questions, on the other hand, need to be deepened, need to become a passion, a force in our lives. A psychological problem is a temporary roadblock. A spiritual question is a lifelong commitment. Suffering born of psychological hang-ups can be cured; suffering arising from our condition as contingent human beings can be deepened and transformed, but not cured. Freud himself put it well when he said that the psychologist's goal is to turn neurotic suffering into ordinary everyday human suffering. It is ordinary everyday human suffering on which turns the lifelong spiritual quest for self-transcendence and transformation.

Psychological growth is in the direction of wisdom, age, grace, maturity, the normal formation process for every human being. Rather than to the formation, spirituality looks to the *trans*formation of human beings. In a homely mixed metaphor, psychological growth makes the human caterpillar tractor into an excellent caterpillar tractor. Spiritual growth transforms the human caterpillar into a butterfly. Psychological maturity sets the human being solidly on the ground of earth. Spiritual maturity opens human beings to their connection with the ground of being. A psychological paragon can be a spiritual dwarf, and a neurotic can be a saint.

Ultimately the difference is a matter of discernment. The practice of *vipassana* will clarify when you are moving in the direction of relief from psychological pain, and when you are engaged in the lifelong commitment to inner spiritual development.

D. God and Self: Identical? or Distinct?

Need the practice of genuine meditation assume a belief in God, and if so, is God identical or distinct from the self?

As noted above, the presentation of the techniques in this book bracketed questions of theology and metaphysics. This is awkward at best, because it's almost impossible to speak of God and reality without making certain assumptions about God and reality. The awkwardness is compounded by the simultaneous use of Buddhist and Christian (sometimes referred to as oriental and western) categories in the presentation of the meditation exercises. So there is a layer of metaphysical ambiguity underlying the psychology/spirituality ambiguities just discussed. This is not the place for a detailed discussion of theodicy and metaphysics. But one can view the broadest division among the interpreters of religious experience as between those who hold to some form of monism (the identity of self and God), and those who hold to some form of dualism (self is not identical with God). In the light of these opposing viewpoints you can begin to choose categories that make the best sense of your religious experience in terms of your own theological and metaphysical commitments.

It is tempting, but not accurate, to contrast the great world religions, placing Hinduism, for example, in the monistic camp, and Christianity in the dualistic. And indeed Hinduism has shown a monistic face to the west in the form of the *Advaita* ("non-dualistic") *Vedanta* school of Hindu thought, with the central insight that *Atman* (Self) is *Brahman* (God). And conversely orthodox Christianity, rejecting pantheism, is at pains to keep a firm distinction between God the creator, on the one hand, and humans who are part of God's creation, on the other.

But the great world religions have at their center the realization that the human mind cannot fully encompass or understand divine truth and reality. They know we must speak of God in metaphors since the reality of God transcends our ordinary experience and images. Beliefs about God are stated in paradoxical ways that fall far short of embodying ultimate truth. Traditional systematic Christian theology for example speaks of God as infinite being. Nothing, including creation, can be outside of God. But in the same breath, it says that creation is distinct from God, and not part of God. So creation is at the same time not outside of God and not part of God. How can this be? The answer lies in an appeal to the metaphor of "sharing" in the divine being. This is the doctrine of "participation." The self participates in the being of God, while at the same time remaining distinct from God. The self has no reality apart from God and yet is not identical with God. Thus the metaphor of participation allows Christians to have their cake (the self is not God: no pantheism) and eat it too (the self shares in the divine being which is infinite and all-embracing). So it is not surprising that a Christian mystic like Meister Eckhart, unconcerned with such theological niceties, interprets his mystical experience in terms that sound like pantheism, so caught up was he with his experience of union, even identity, with God.

On the other hand, Hindu interpretations of reality are not all of them pantheistic. Yoga philosophy, for example, sees a dualism between the ego embodied in the changing world of nature (the changing principle is called *prakriti*) and the unchanging divine self (the principle of *purusha*) whose realization is the goal of life.

The harder you come down on the side of monism, the more likely you are to regard the world of history and nature as an illusory veil hiding you from the vision of God, the one true reality. The harder you come down on the side of dualism, the more likely you are to water down the ineffable mystery of God's transcendence in your effort to give worth and esteem to the world of creation and history. So there is a perennial ongoing dialectic between theologies of transcendence and theologies of incarnation. In the current winds of fashion the latter are in the ascendancy, exemplified by the incarnational theology of Matthew Fox and the liberation theologies of Latin American theologians.

A final alternative would be to cast your lot with so-called negative theology, best expressed by Thomas Aquinas, "We can know what God is not; we cannot know what God is." Negative theology involves three logical steps. First, we observe love and knowledge and goodness and being in ourselves, and so we conclude that these qualities must be in God as well. Second, we recognize that in God these qualities are without any of the limits or shortcomings which they have in human beings, so "we know what God is not": God is not limited. In God these qualities exist in the highest possible degree and without limit: limitless love, infinite knowledge, supreme being. Finally we realize that such infinite qualities exceed all capacity of our minds to understand. We have no idea what infinite love looks like, how infinite knowledge works, or what supreme reality is in itself: "we do not know what God is." Such then is negative theology. Attempts to describe God in positive experiential terms leave one speechless.

Many have seen a kinship between such negative theology and the apparent "agnosticism" with which the Buddhist speaks of the transcendent state of *nirvana*. *Nirvana* is the state of enlightenment where there is detachment, where there is a letting go of all grasping, craving, and *self*ishness. Indeed there is no self in the sense of a separate ego you can hang on to. So the Buddhist talks not of *atman* (self) but of *anatman* (no-self), akin to the teaching of Jesus that the only way to find yourself is to lose yourself. So when the Buddhist interprets mystical experience you will hear of no-self and of a transrational mystical state of *nirvana* about which nothing can be said.

The viewpoint of apophatic theology—theology without words—is very friendly to *vipassana* meditation, in which the rational mind is occupied so that the spirit may find itself empty and open to contact with transcendence. This contact is without words, without images. It is often experienced as a blank, as nothingness, a nothingness that is somehow mysteriously full, but in no nameable way.

So to get back to the original question: *Need the practice of genuine meditation assume a belief in God?* The answer of apophatic theology is "No"—not in a God who can be named. In this spirit, orthodox Jews to this day will not write the name of God. A God who can be named is a god reduced, an idol. But unlike the psychologism discussed above, genuine spiritual meditation is open to a transcendent realm in some sense of the word, however mysterious it may be.

And to the second part of the question: *And if so, is God*

identical or distinct from the self? For the monist, the self is identical with God. For the dualist, the self is distinct from God. The theologian sensitive to the paradoxes of human efforts to grasp transcendence will answer, "Both." The apophatic theologian will answer, "Neither."

IV. Suggestions for Further Reading

A. Criteria

There is no shortage of books on meditation. Consider typical bookstore inventories. Religious bookstores favor devotional literature on prayer and meditation presented strictly from a parochial point of view. General trade bookstores offer meditation books in the religion and self-improvement departments. In these stores popular oriental sects are the generally favored religions, and the self-improvement category is characterized by visualization and auto-hypnosis techniques for resolving various problems of addiction and life-adjustment. In New Age bookstores, the majority of the inventory is made up of books on explorations of consciousness including meditation. Here you will find literature in all of the above categories. You will also find manuals representing the teachings of various human potential groups, and meditation guides not only from the great world religions but from each of their branches and denominations. New Age bookstores also thrive on occult and esoteric literature, including witchcraft, astral projection, aura reading, channeling, healing, ESP, crystal reading, and so forth without end, many of which areas can be considered under the aegis of "meditation." In the midst of this abundance and variety the challenge is not to come up with a long list of suggested readings, but with a short list. So here is my short list of very special books.

From this cornucopia of consciousness techniques, I am concerned to separate the authentic from the superstitious, and the unique from the banal. I have looked for treatments that are critical rather than gullible, and ecumenical rather than confessional. These criteria make for the following short list.

B. Suggested Readings

Anthony, Dick, Bruce Ecker, and Ken Wilber (editors). *Spiritual Choices: The Problem of Recognizing Authentic Paths to Inner Transformation.* New York: Paragon House Publishers, 1987.

Psychologist Dick Anthony, under the auspices of the Department of Psychiatry at the University of North Carolina (Chapel Hill), developed a typology for assessing spiritual and consciousness groups as a framework for presenting his research on the mental health effects of the new religions. The typology is used to assess the content of interviews with Werner Erhard (EST), Ram Dass (Hindu), Claudio Naranjo (Tibetan Buddhist), and Steven Tipton (on Zen), among others. And there is a series of essays giving a transpersonal psychological evaluation of contemporary spiritual and consciousness groups. This book suggests criteria and models for a field in much need of further research.

de Mello, S.J., Anthony. *Sadhana: A Way to God (Christian Exercises in Eastern Form)*. St. Louis: The Institute of Jesuit Sources, 1978.

This work has become a classic. *Sadhana* is a Hindu word meaning spiritual exercise, discipline, or technique. De Mello enriches the *Spiritual Exercises* of St. Ignatius with Hindu meditation forms. The book includes Awareness, Fantasy, and Devotional exercises. Especially valuable is his explanation of the connection between Awareness and Spiritual Contemplation.

Enomiya-Lassalle, Hugo. *Living in the New Consciousness*. Boston: Shambhala Publications, Inc., 1988.

A German Jesuit who has been teaching at Sophia University in Japan since 1929, Hugo Lassalle discovered Zen for Christianity. A world renowned scholar in the history of Zen Buddhism, he became a practitioner of Zen meditation in 1943, and is acknowledged as a Zen Master. This collection from his books and unpublished writings and speeches communicates the significance of the new consciousness—non-dualistic awareness—for the future course of human evolution.

Fox, Matthew. *Meditations with Meister Eckhart.* Santa Fe: Bear and Co., Inc., 1982.

Matthew Fox, a Dominican creation theologian, has arranged and adapted the writings of medieval mystic Meister Eckhart (c. 1260-1329) into a series of meditations. Eckhart's spiritual genius was able to break out of the culture of Christendom to express mystical insight in universal accents so that Hindus and Buddhists claim him as one of their own and Jung and Fromm call him teacher.

Green, Barry, with W. Timothy Gallwey. *The Inner Game of Music.* New York: Doubleday/Anchor Press, 1986.

This is the first book that applied the "inner game" principles of natural learning to an area other than sports. Green applies Gallwey's "inner game of tennis" methods to the teaching/ learning of musical expression. He reports only those techniques that survived the test of years of experimenting with students. The book is a testimony to the *practical* power of awareness in transforming human behavior. It has applications far beyond music.

Goleman, Daniel. *The Meditative Mind: The Varieties of Meditative Experience.* Los Angeles: Tarcher Press, 1988.

This modern version of William James' *The Varieties of Religious Experience* takes a world religions approach to meditation experience. Goleman gives an overview of different types of meditation techniques in both east and west. He examines the distinct levels of consciousness that result from their practice on a continuing basis.

Johnston, William. *The Mirror Mind: Spirituality and Transformation.* San Francisco: Harper and Row, 1981.

This is another book that has become a classic. With great empathy for Buddhism, Johnston, a Christian professor at Sophia University in Japan, initiates a Christian-Buddhist dialogue. With a view to their mutual enrichment, he compares the approaches of the two religions to self-realization, transformation, healing, meditation, death and love.

Miller, William R., and John E. Martin (editors). *Behavior Therapy and Religion: Integrating Spiritual and Behavioral Approaches to Change.* Newbury Park: Sage Publications, Inc., 1988.

Carl Rogers, Karl Menninger, Rollo May, Carl Jung, Gordon Allport, Erik Erikson, Viktor Frankl, Lawrence Kohlberg, and Erich Fromm are psychologists and personality theorists who recognize how central to human development are religion and spirituality. But behavioral psychologists have remained uninterested, if not hostile to such a role for spirituality. The contributors take a hard-nosed look at how to incorporate religion and spirituality effectively in clinical behavioral contexts.

Murphy, Michael, and Steven Donovan. *The Physical and Psychological Effects of Meditation: A Review of Contemporary Meditation Research.* San Rafael: Esalen Institute, 1988.

This monograph contains over one thousand bibliographic references and it reviews seven hundred studies of the profound effects that meditation has on the mind and body. The focus is on the physiology and psychology of what happens during and after meditation sessions. We look forward to the day when a similar monograph can be written on the use of meditation as a tool of research rather than as an object of research.

Ornstein, Robert, and Paul Ehrlich. *New World New Mind: Moving Toward Conscious Evolution.* New York: Doubleday, 1989.

Robert Ornstein, president of the Institute for the Study of Human Knowledge, and biologist Paul Ehrlich join forces in a

futurist critique of how present modes of consciousness training have fallen dangerously behind the present course of scientific and cultural change. Our minds' default responses are set
for a world that no longer exists. They propose a curriculum of
spiritual techniques applicable to the character and pace of the
world that does exist.

Notes

1. Calcutta, 1968, cited in *The Bulletin of the North American Board for East-West Dialogue* (January 1989), p. 1.

2. Cited in an interview in "Meditation of Consciousness," *Noetic Sciences Review* (Autumn 1988), p. 20.

3. The techniques in this book are quite traditional, not novel, nor would I want them to be. The Mind/Body/Breathing exercises were originally inspired by Anthony de Mello's presentation in *Sadhana: A Way to God* (St. Louis: Institute of Jesuit Sources, 1978). I found it more useful to give them a Buddhist rather than a Hindu slant. And the interspersed suggestions and applications are targeted to inexperienced practitioners, rather than to the religious community audience envisioned by de Mello.

4. "Meditation and Consciousness," *Noetic Sciences Review* (Autumn 1988), p. 16.

5. Buddhist text from the *Saraha*, cited by Ram Dass, *Journey of Awareness*, p. 30.

6. Arnold Mindell, *Dreambody: The Body's Role in Revealing the Self* (Santa Monica: Sigo Press, 1982), p. 160.

7. *Ibid.*, p. 193.

8. Gerald May, *Will and Spirit* (San Francisco: Harper, 1982), p. 316.

9. Anthony de Mello, S. J., *Sadhana: A Way to God* (St. Louis: The Institute of Jesuit Sources, 1978), p. 37.

10. Herbert Otto, *Ways of Growth*, p. 27.

11. *The Living Flame of Love.*

12. Elaine Partnow (ed.), *The Quotable Woman* (Anchor/Doubleday, 1978).

13. Raymond Blackney, M. E., *Meister Eckhart: A Modern Translation*, p. 9.

14. Raymond Smullyan, *This Book Needs No Title* (New York: Simon and Schuster, 1980), p. 139.

15. Anthony de Mello, *Sadhana: A Way to God* (St. Louis: Institute of Jesuit Studies, 1978), p. 24.

16. Cited in Marianne S. Andersen and Louis M. Savary, *Passages* (Harper and Row, 1972), p. 217.

17. *Ibid.*, p. 53.

18. Anthony de Mello, *Sadhana: A Way to God* (St. Louis: Institute of Jesuit Studies, 1978), p. 24.

19. Joseph Goldstein and Jack Kornfield, *Seeking the Heart of Wisdom: The Path of Insight Meditation* (Boulder: Shambhala Publications, 1987), p. 56.

20. Peter Michael Hamel, *Through Music to the Self* (Boulder: Shambhala, 1979), p. 120.

21. Robert Ornstein and Paul Ehrlich, *New World, New Mind: Moving Toward Conscious Evolution* (New York: Doubleday, 1989), p. 148.

22. Marion Mountain, *The Zen Environment*, p. 96.

23. Matthew Fox, *Meditations with Meister Eckhart* (Santa Fe: Bear and Co., 1982), p. 61.

24. *Zen Without Zen Masters*, p. 32.

25. "The Way of Transcending Action," *Yoga Journal* (March/April 1989), p. 120.

26. *The Mirror Mind* (Harper, 1981), p. 36.

27. Thomas Merton, as cited in *Passages*, p. 223.

28. Cited by George Will's syndicated column (December 20, 1983).

29. Zen story as cited by Paul Reps (ed.), *Zen Flesh, Zen Bones* (New York: Doubleday, 1961), p. 32.

30. Cited in Andersen *et al.*, *Passages* (Harper, 1972), p. 180.

31. Piero Ferrucci, *What We May Be* (Los Angeles: Tarcher, 1982), p. 77.

32. *Yoga and Zen* (Routledge and Kegan Paul, 1983), pp. 39–40.

33. Cited by William James, *The Varieties of Religious Experience* (New York: New American Library, 1958), p. 292.

34. Cited by Andersen and Savary in *Passages* (Harper and Row, 1972), p. 180.

35. Cited by Stewart Brand, *The Media Lab* (New York: Penguin Books, 1988), p. 3.

36. William Johnston, *The Mirror Mind*, p. 94.

37. Needleman, *Lost Christianity*, p. 177.

38. Anthony de Mello, *Sadhana: A Way to God* (St. Louis: Institute of Jesuit Sources, 1978), pp. 61–62. This technique is inspired by Exercise 15 in *Sadhana*, entitled, "Here and There."

39. Peter's quotes, p. 199.

40. I acknowledge my debt to Robert Fritz, founder of the DMA organization devoted to the study and implementation of human creativity. Workshops taken with DMA have influenced this book's approach to decision-making and to the relationships among the different levels of human consciousness. For a full exposition of DMA, see Robert Fritz, *The Path of Least Resistance* (Salem: DMA, 1984, and the expanded and revised edition, Fawcett Columbine Book, 1989).

41. Piero Ferrucci, *What We May Be* (Los Angeles: Tarcher, 1982), p. 77.

42. As quoted by Raymond Smullyan, *This Book Needs No Title* (New York: Touchstone, 1980), p. 135.

43. Fred Morris, *Hypnosis with Friends and Lovers* (San Francisco: Harper and Row, 1979), p. 10.

44. The balance of this technique is adapted from Dr. Massimo Rosselli, following Ferrucci in *What We May Be*, pp. 82–83.

45. Cited by W. H. Auden and Louis Kronenberger in *The Viking Book of Aphorisms* (Dorset Press, 1981), p. 236.

46. *Daybreak* (New York: The Dial Press, 1968).

47. Dick Anthony, Bruce Ecker, and Ken Wilber (eds.), *Spiritual Choices* (New York: Paragon House, 1987), p. 1.

48. Cited in *Noetic Sciences Review* (Summer 1988), p. 1.